NO COST/LOW COST INVESTING

NO COST/ LOW COST INVESTING

CHET CURRIER
DAVID SMYTH

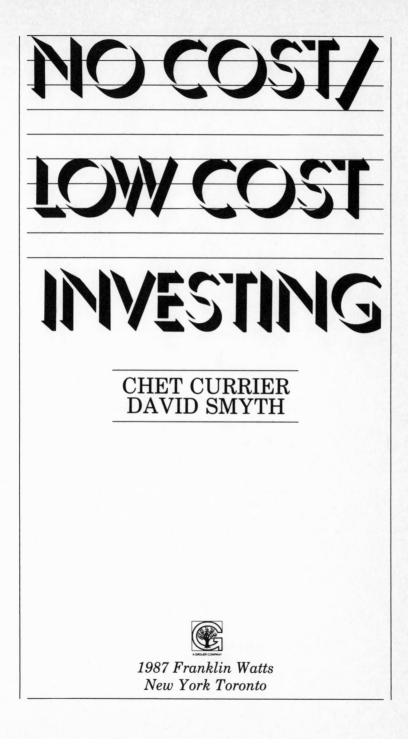

A GROLIER COMPANY

1987 Franklin Watts
New York Toronto

Library of Congress Cataloging-in-Publication Data

Currier, Chet.
No cost/low cost investing.

Includes index.
1. Investments—United States. 2. Securities—United
States. I. Smyth, David, 1929–   . II. Title.
III. Title: Low cost investing.
HG4910.C86 1987   332.6'78   87-13690
ISBN 0-531-15527-7

C O N T E N T S

or at the most one small commission on your initial
purchase of one share.

CHAPTER 3 · Mutual Funds

*No-load mutual funds may seem a better bargain
than load funds. But even no-loads can nick you 2%
or more a year in hidden charges, fees, and expenses.
Do you know which funds charge the least? And do
you know why they are usually the best-performing
funds year after year?*

CHAPTER 4 · Closed-End Funds

*While the herd buys mutual funds, a select group of
savvy investors passes them by to invest in the little-
known closed-end funds. Why? Because you can
sometimes buy them at a large discount and sell them
later at a big premium over their net asset value.*

CHAPTER 5 · U.S. Government Securities

*Do you know who will sell you absolutely
top-flight securities without charging you a penny
in commissions? Pay you interest in advance?
Give you a tax break? Good old Uncle Sam.*

CHAPTER 6 · Banking

*Banks would dearly love to have you transact all your
business with them through a teller machine. It saves*

NO COST/LOW COST INVESTING

INTRODUCTION

THE FINANCIAL SERVICES MAZE

For all of us with money to manage and invest, this is the age of "financial services." You may, if you choose, buy and sell stocks through the bank where you have your checking account, or pay bills with checks written on your account at a stock brokerage firm. Bankers and brokers, along with life insurance companies, mutual fund organizations, credit unions, and so forth—all are blurring into a single giant industry offering products that resemble each other more and more. On top of that, there is a new breed of "experts"—financial planners and accountants—bidding for the privilege of advising you on what choices to make.

This is all to the good, you may say. It came about because the once-rigid world of finance has been deregulated, opening the windows to a refreshing breeze of increased competition. It allows you more options and greater flexibility in trying to make your money grow. But let's stop for a moment and consider why Sears Roebuck and the Prudential and American Express and Merrill Lynch and Fidelity and so many others are devoting so much effort to wooing you.

The answer isn't complicated. They see a chance to make big money in the financial services game.

By all means, let's not begrudge them that motive. It's nothing more nor less than capitalism, the American way of making things happen. But let's also not misunderstand what they are up to. Much of the money they make comes from commissions, fees, markups and markdowns, sales charges, management charges, custodial charges. And whence does all this revenue arise? From the pockets of the customer. To paraphrase cartoonist Walt Kelly, "He is us."

Sure, it is generally accepted that some costs are inevitable in the business of investing. If a broker suggests a stock that turns a 100% profit, do we think it unfair that the broker takes a 5% or 10% cut? The owners of the horse that won the Kentucky Derby a couple of years ago put it simply: You've got to Spend a Buck to make a buck.

Yet over time, a sales charge here, an annual account fee there, and you can find yourself getting nicked to death. The fact is, there are ways to minimize some of the important costs of investing and to eliminate a good many others altogether. That's what this book is all about. The pages that follow describe numerous methods by which you can lower the house odds against you whenever you try to put your money to work, whether your goals are ambitious or conservative.

We'll discuss ways to reduce commissions by dealing with a discount broker, or by negotiating the cost with a full-service broker. We'll tell you how to accumulate a portfolio of stocks at little or no commission cost, and perhaps even at below-market prices, through dividend reinvestment plans. There is nothing really new or secret about these DRI programs, but an astonishingly large percentage of the people who could benefit from them are not taking advantage of the opportunity. Few brokers or other intermediaries are about to enlighten them.

Next we'll discuss how to lighten the cost burden of investing in mutual funds, and why the term "no-load" doesn't necessarily mean "no-cost" or even "low-cost" any more. From a small backwater of the investment business a few decades ago, the fund industry has truly grown to big-time status. As of 1987, the number of funds surpassed the total of all the common stocks listed on the New York Stock Exchange. With all that growth, however, an old disparity still exists within the business. Some funds are set up to appeal specifically to investors who are alert and savvy enough to seek out low-cost opportunities; others seem to exist almost solely for the benefit of those who sponsor and market them. Since funds of both types may pursue virtually identical goals and own the same kinds of securities, it is obviously essential to be able to tell the difference.

While we're on the subject of funds, we'll take a look at an intriguing proposition that often arises with little fanfare: the chance to buy into a portfolio of stocks or bonds at a price well below its current market value. This occurs when a "closed-end," or publicly traded, investment company is changing hands in the marketplace for less than its net asset value. Sometimes this "discount," as it is called, represents a real bargain; other times it simply betokens questionable merchandise.

Then we'll shift gears to examine the biggest seller of no-cost/low-cost investments, the United States government. Many people who want the safety and yield offered by Treasury bonds, notes, and bills pay a banker, broker, or fund manager to handle the details for them. With a little initiative and energy, however, you can cut out the attendant commissions and management fees by dealing directly with Uncle Sam.

Next, we'll delve into the many mysteries of some of our most familiar financial institutions—commercial banks and their close relatives, savings banks and savings and loans. Perhaps nowhere else in the financial world are the effects of deregulation and new technology so manifest. We have automatic teller machines, banking by telephone, banking by home computer, bank mergers and, yes, bank failures (more of the latter lately than at any time since the Depression of the 1930s). An interior designer we know has made a nice living in the past several years just redecorating branch offices of savings banks in the New York City area as the names on the doors changed. In this climate of decay and rebirth, bank fees and charges have proliferated like mosquitoes in a swamp.

Lastly, we'll evaluate the no-cost/low-cost investment opportunities that may be available to you through your employer, such as pension and profit-sharing programs and stock ownership plans. Like most of the other ideas discussed in this book, these vehicles won't transport you to the land of instant wealth. At the same time, they may represent some of the best deals you can find anywhere. An employee of the venerable General Electric Co. told recently of having made regular purchases of GE stock through a company plan. For a good many years, she said, she pursued this endeavor without much sense of gratification. When the price of GE stock soared in the 1980s, she got paid handsomely for her patience.

In devoting so much attention to the costs of investing, what is our purpose? Don't we run the risk of entangling ourselves in trivia when we should be keeping the big picture fixed in our minds? Well, yes, perhaps. Nobody wants to spend too much time counting pennies when pounds are at stake. But as we have said, those pennies can add up to a lot of money spent rather than invested, working to enrich somebody else rather than you.

From our experience and observation, we think most people err on the side of paying too little attention to investment costs, not too much. The last time you bought or sold a stock, did you calculate what the commission amounted to as a percentage of the total value of the transaction? How much, in dollars, does your mutual fund subtract from your account each year to cover management fees and operating costs?

In most cases, the system is set up to keep such matters from troubling you much. A mutual fund, for example, must disclose its management fees in percentage terms, say, 0.75 of 1% per year. We have never seen a mutual fund statement, however, that had an entry reading: **In the past year, fees and expenses reduced the value of your account by $_____.**

The last time you ran low on checks, did you bother to ask anyone the price of a new box of checks before you sent in the convenient reorder form? The form says nothing about price per check, and you never get a separate bill to pay when the new supply arrives in the mail. The charge will show up on next month's bank statement, of course. By then will you remember how many checks were in the package? If you do, you may be surprised at how much you paid, possibly even angry. Still, the amount involved may not seem worth the trouble of complaining, of seeking some cheaper alternative the next time. After all, how often do you order new checks?

From this you might deduce that check printing is a good business to be in—and you'd be right. The net profits reported by Deluxe Check Printers Inc., the dominant company in the industry, grew from $24.1 million in 1976 to $104.2 million in 1985, or at an average rate of 18.5% a year, according to the Value Line Investment Survey. A competitor, John H. Harland Co., had earnings growth of 21.5 percent a year over the same period.

Again, no complaint. As investors we like the profit motive and admire those who act on it successfully. Anyone who owned Deluxe or Harland stock in that ten-year period got a nice piece of the action in checks (both stocks increased in value more than tenfold). But we're not going to be naive about the system. It has its flaws, its built-in conflicts of interest that often pit investor and intermediary in adversarial roles. So it is that an unabashed capitalist like Alan Abelson of *Barron's* magazine can say of the stock market: "It offers rewards to risk-takers and even greater rewards to those who take the risk-takers."

Nothing personal, but we need to be wary of full-service stockbrokers because the system requires us to be wary. They are supposed to be our agents, our representatives. Yet the system doesn't pay them directly on the basis of how well they represent us. Instead, it compensates them on the basis of the quantity and type of merchandise they sell us. If you deal very much with brokers, it behooves you to consider the transactions you conduct from their point of view. And if there are alternatives to paying full brokerage commissions, it behooves you to investigate those alternatives.

If the idea of no-cost/low-cost investing needed a boost of any kind, it got one from Congress in the Tax Reform Act of 1986. Among many other changes in the U.S. tax system, that law provides that many investment expenses that used to be fully deductible on income tax returns now count as "miscellaneous" expenses that aren't deducted until they exceed 2% of your income. On top of that, deductions for many types of interest expenses are being reduced by stages to zero. To a great extent, Uncle Sam has just stopped helping us pay our investment and money management bills.

The point of no-cost/low-cost investing isn't to be stingy or small-minded. It is to strive to get the most out of every investment dollar you can afford to set aside. Beyond the obvious cost benefits, we believe this approach has another virtue to recommend it. Taking a no-cost/low-cost approach means developing a large measure of self-reliance and healthy skepticism toward those who would provide you with "financial services."

Operating that way, you must develop a system of some sort, a plan from which you don't want to deviate much. So you are less likely to be tempted by hot tips or by the glossy package of merchandise some financial services marketer has put together to feature in this month's inventory clearance or sales contest. That adds up to discipline, a valuable asset for just about any investor in any financial season.

C H A P T E R

1

**BROKERS
AND
DISCOUNT
BROKERS**

Brokers

For most of us, the business of investing and trying to make our money grow means dealing with a broker—a specialized professional who has access to the merchandise we want, and who can serve us as an adviser, confidante, and cheerleader in our efforts. Actually, within the ranks of any given securities firm, there are "brokers" of many different types: executives who run the firm itself; people who handle orders for the firm at stock exchanges and in other securities markets; the institutional sales force, which deals only with money managers for pension funds, mutual funds, and the like; traders who buy and sell securities with the firm's own money; and so-called retail brokers who deal with the public.

This last group, obviously, is the one we're concerned with. They used to be known generally as registered representatives, the name signifying that they had passed qualifying tests given by major securities exchanges and were registered with those exchanges. These days, they are most often called account executives. They are hardly ever referred to as salesmen or salespeople. Yet selling is in fact the job their employers pay them to do. The most successful of them are known in the industry as "big producers," as measured not by their financial acumen but by the amount of gross commission revenues they bring in. One can succeed as a retail broker by attracting a large and loyal clientele through hard work, diligent research, and a keen sense of investment planning and timing. One can also succeed as a retail broker by having rich relatives who keep all their business in the family.

Our intention here is neither to praise brokers nor to vilify them. We simply want to try to understand them, what they can and cannot do, and how they make their living, so that we can deal with them intelligently and pay them only what we need to pay them in order to pursue our financial goals. A central thesis of this book is that brokers and other intermediaries, however useful, are not always necessary. In this and the next two chapters, we will tell you how you can buy and sell stocks or mutual fund shares at lower cost than a "full-service" broker wants to charge you, or indeed at no cost whatsoever.

To start with, let's consider a typical stock market investment. Your broker, Otto "Pay Me" Moore, has been urging you for some time to buy shares of the stock of KBI Industries, which his firm's research department is touting as a buy for both the short and long term. After reading the report Moore has sent you, you decide to go for it and instruct him to buy you 300 shares at the market, that is, at the best price his firm can get. Shortly after the stock market opens the next day, Moore calls to tell you that you have acquired those 300 shares at a price of $20 each. He asks you to send him a check for the $6,000 cost of buying the stock plus a commission of $145. The commission is not stated as a percentage of the amount invested. A little quick mathematics, however, tells you that it is just under 2.5%.

What does Otto get out of this? That depends on the details of his firm's compensation schedule, and probably on his own standing within the firm as well. If he is a young, struggling broker who has not yet brought enough money into the firm to pay for the considerable cost of training him, his take might be, oh, $50. If he is a powerhouse "producer" coveted by every major firm on Wall Street, it might be closer to $100. Moore's piece of the action might also be increased if KBI is an over-the-counter stock in which his firm "makes a market." Pay systems in the securities business can be quite complicated; in any case, you know that you have had to spend $145 in order to get the stock. When it comes time to sell it, you can expect to pay another commission of about the same size.

Who decides what this commission charge is going to be? In theory, at least, it is a matter for open negotiation between you and any broker with whom you might deal. As only a small and occasional customer of Moore's, you probably won't get far haggling with him. "It's against our firm's policy," he might tell you in a polite but final tone of voice. If, on the other hand, you were a high roller who had paid orthodontia bills over the years for all five of Moore's children, you might be surprised at how flexible that "policy" could be.

Important customer or not, you have other options besides accepting whatever commission rate Moore and his employer set. Suppose you liked KBI stock without the persuasion of a bullish research report. You might seek out a discount brokerage firm that would charge you a commission of $80, $60, even $40 for the same transaction. Or a little investigation might lead you to the information that KBI itself will sell you stock, commission-free, through its dividend reinvestment plan. The next time you see Moore, at a PTA meeting, you raise the subject of these alternatives, trying to be as tactful as possible.

Moore listens calmly, showing no sign that you have ruffled his feathers. In his line of work, he hears this stuff all the time, and his reply is well practiced. "Absolutely," he says. "There are lots of places with lower commission rates than mine. But you're getting full value, and more, for the money you invest with me. KBI was my suggestion, wasn't it? Nobody else on the Street covers the company the way our analyst does. And I'm keeping my eye on the stock for you. What did it close at today—20⅝? We've already covered the commission and we're making money."

All in all, a pretty disarming little speech. You and he—"we," as he so judiciously put it—are partners in a venture that is paying off for both parties. Should KBI decline in price, the chances are good that Otto will be there to commiserate, to assure that you haven't made a serious mistake after all. The investment is merely taking longer than expected to produce its prospective profit. Should the stock go down and stay down, he'll also be more than ready with ideas of how to make the loss work to your best advantage for tax purposes, and to point you toward a new idea that will put you back on a winning course.

But let's suppose that you have set objectives for yourself that are more specific than "making money." The plan you have developed calls for buying and accumulating stocks, not dodging in and out of the market as some adviser comes up with new suggestions. You're willing, able, and pleased to develop your own selections and strategies, so you don't need most of the services your friend Moore is selling in a package. All you require is an order-taker. And that makes you a prime candidate for a discount broker or, perhaps even better, a dividend reinvestment plan.

Investors didn't always have such a choice. For most

of the long history of the American securities industry, all brokers operated under a schedule of fixed minimum commission rates for all transactions. So whether you wanted extensive advice and hand-holding as you bought and sold, or simply wanted an order to be carried out, you paid the same "full-service" rate. Many observers saw a special irony in this situation. Here was Wall Street, the bastion of free enterprise, operating under a special set of rules that shielded it from the rough and tumble of price competition. When such competition was proposed, there were many industry leaders protesting that an end to "fixed rates" would create havoc within the markets and in the nation's capital-raising mechanism. Eventually, the authorities decreed that fixed rates would end on May 1, 1975, and that brokerage firms could thereafter charge whatever commissions the market would bear—"negotiated rates."

On Wall Street, the event was dubbed Mayday—a nice play on the double meaning of the word. Once Mayday arrived, negotiation of commission rates began in earnest. This negotiation, however, took distinctly different forms for the small, individual investor and for the big investing institutions such as pension funds, insurance companies, bank trust departments, and mutual funds. Then, as now, the institutions were taking an increasingly dominant role in the marketplace (at this writing, block trades of 10,000 shares or more—a measure of institutional trading—account for about half of all the activity that takes place on the New York Stock Exchange). They were and are Wall Street's most important customers. So money managers employed by these institutions found themselves in a strong position to bargain for lower commission rates. What's more, their lawyers advised them that, in their capacities as fiduciaries (managers of other people's money), they were probably bound morally and legally to push for the lowest rates possible. The typical Wall Street firm could ill afford to lose their business, and so it went right along.

The circumstances were especially rough on a category of brokerage firms known as "research boutiques," which specialized in providing institutions with sophisticated analysis and financial information in return for commission business. Most of these boutiques merged with other firms or went out of business.

For the big diversified investment houses, however, Mayday was no disaster. While commission rates for institutions were tumbling, they found that they could hold rates for their individual customers steady or even increase them. For the small investor, with his lack of clout, the "negotiating" was done largely by the broker. The situation wasn't entirely one-sided, though. It created an opening for a new breed of investment firm known as a discount broker, and discounters in increasing numbers jumped in to fill that opening.

Discount Brokers

The original idea behind discount brokerage was much like the approach adopted by the first discounters in the consumer retailing business. It was no-frills service at a no-frills price. The discount firms employed no brokers or other commissioned salespeople at all. They were manned by salaried staffers who solicited no business and made no recommendations, but merely took orders and had them executed. They used advertising to gain attention, and they competed on price (while asserting that their customers still got fast, courteous, and efficient service).

More than a decade later, the discount brokerage business has become much more diverse. There is no way today to describe the typical discount brokerage firm. Many, especially the smaller operations, still concentrate on promoting the commission savings they offer. A sampling of them can be found in any issue of many financial publications. Others, however, have expanded into such fields as individual retirement accounts, trading by home computer, and too many others to list here. One idea that has proved quite popular with discounters' customers, in fact, is just the opposite of the "discount" service. For a small commission charge, the firm handles dealings in no-load mutual funds. To pay a commission to buy fund shares when you could do it yourself at no charge is hardly our idea of no-cost/low-cost investing. Yet, for the sake of convenience alone, many investors evidently find that it is worth the price. We won't presume to pass any judgment on these people, but we also don't plan to join them in that particular pursuit.

Thanks to their growth and proliferation, discount brokers today are easy to find. Chances are there is one as close to you as a nearby bank or branch of a savings institution, with all the convenience that that implies. National firms that specialize in the business typically have toll-free "800" phone numbers that make it easy (and no-cost to boot) to open an account and transact business. But how to choose a given firm to deal with is a more complicated story.

"The range of pricing variation among discount brokers is enormous—much greater than conventional brokers," said Mark Coler, president of Discount Brokerage Advisory Services (72 Fifth Avenue, New York, NY 10011), a firm that tracks developments in the industry. "Having studied every discount commission schedule in the country that my firm could lay its collective hands on, I can state categorically that there is no such thing as the best discount broker—or the cheapest," Coler wrote in the American Association of Individual Investors publication *The AAII Journal.*

Coler divides discounters into two distinct groups. One, which he calls "valuebrokers," sets its commission rates in much the same way that traditional full-service brokers do, calculating them based on the dollar value of a given trade. The other, which he speaks of as "sharebrokers," sets its rates according to the number of shares being bought or sold. "A sharebroker who charges per unit is generally cheaper if you are buying higher-priced stocks," he observed. "Valuebrokers, on the other hand, are cheaper if you deal mostly in low-priced stocks. If you are an active trader and deal in both types of trades, you may want to consider setting up two different brokerage accounts."

Naturally, there are questions other than price that must carry a lot of weight when you decide whether and how to use any given discount brokerage firm. Poor service, if you should encounter it, isn't worth any amount of commission savings. You might opt to do business at a local bank or savings institution, even though its rates are well above rock-bottom, for the convenience of a ready link to your checking and savings accounts, or for any of several other reasons. Or experience may give you a preference for a firm that you think does the best job of executing trades. No matter what sort of broker you are dealing with, good execution is vitally important.

Suppose you wanted to buy 600 shares of KBI and, as an experiment, split the order in two between a full-service broker and a discounter. Carefully synchronizing your actions, you and a confederate give each firm simultaneous orders to buy 300 shares at the market. Let's say the full-service broker gets you the stock at $20 for a $145 commission, and the discounter obtains it at 20¼, or $20.25, with a commission of $70. Which one got you the better deal? By our reckoning, it's a dead heat. Your cost in both cases is $6,145. We hasten to add that this example is not intended to suggest that full-service brokers, on the average, do any better execution work than discounters do. Says Coler of the discount brokerage industry, "The trades are executed just as quickly, and in the same manner as trades from all other brokers." All we are trying to suggest is that commission rates don't tell the whole story of what it costs to do business with a broker. Nevertheless, if you are an absolute demon on the subject of commission rates (surely a respectable attitude for any militant no-cost/low-cost investor), Coler's firm publishes and sells periodic lists of his ratings of the "least expensive discounters" for several representative stock transactions.

In the hypothetical test trade we described at the beginning of the previous paragraph, we used both a full-service and a discount broker. That suggests an idea that might be worth expanding on. Why not maintain accounts at both types of firms, using each when it is to our greatest benefit to do so? No question, occasions can arise when even the most sophisticated investor is better off in the hands of a full-service broker rather than a discounter. For instance, let's say you want to buy one share of a $25 stock as a symbolic gift for a grade school niece. Even discount brokers set minimum commissions per trade of, say, $35 that would make such a stock purchase too expensive to be worth the trouble. Your friend Moore, on the other hand, might have both the inclination and the necessary authority to handle the order without commission as a courtesy, chalking up the costs to the building of goodwill. In general, the cost savings that can be realized in dealing with a discount broker are most apparent for people who are regular, active investors. If you buy or sell only in small amounts once or twice a year, you will probably be best served by choosing a broker for quality of service rather than seeking to save a whole lot on commissions.

But back to the plan we were hatching. You'll want to keep doing some of your business with Otto Moore, so that he will keep priming your pump with ideas (not to mention an occasional pep talk). In addition, you are hoping that sometime soon he will see fit to get you in on some of the hot "new issue" stock offerings in which his firm participates. It's not realistic to expect that a discount broker can do that for you.

While you keep up the relationship with Moore,

however, you also plan to pare down your commission expenses by sending the "easy business" through your discount brokerage account. That way you'll get the best of both worlds.

It's a crafty plan, no doubt about it, but it won't work if you get too greedy. Your chum Moore is going to get wise to it very quickly. If he chats with you on the phone, suggesting ideas and sending you research reports, he isn't going to be happy at all if you act on the ideas but give your orders to somebody else. To be fair about it, his anger will be thoroughly justified. After all, he's working on your behalf and you are not paying him for his trouble. Too many clients like you, and he'll be out of a job. Can't you find some other full-service broker when his patience runs out? Of course. But sooner or later any broker will dope you out as a problem customer, and you'll be back where you started.

At this point, in fact, it might be instructive to take a few minutes to consider the broker's way of life—not, by any means, in a pass-the-hat bid for sympathy, but just so we know whom we're dealing with. If Moore is like many a real-life broker, he has to do a lot of hustling. His firm pressures him hard to meet certain numbers, i.e., at least $150,000 or $200,000 in gross commissions each year. If he can't do that, the employer may tell him, either implicitly or explicitly, it would like to give his telephone, his desk, and his stock quotation terminal to someone who can do better.

If he doesn't have a solid base of customers who buy his wares regularly, and in turn provide him with new customers through referrals, he probably also makes a lot of "cold calls." Maybe he has been able to lay his hands on a nearby corporation's executive roster, or the alumni directory from some upper-crust university. On Monday morning he starts with the A's—"Abercrombie, Ackerman, Agnelli. . . ." No matter how diligent he is in his work, he most likely has his share of disgruntled customers fond of calling him and writing him about their grievances, real or imagined.

All right, you may say, that's what selling is like, no matter what line of goods you're peddling. If he can't stand those pressures, he should be in some other line of work. You'd have a point. An acquaintance of ours started out some years ago selling life insurance, with only lists of people he didn't know and a guidebook to cold-calling that the insurance company had thoughtfully provided when he went through its training program. Going by that book, he would introduce himself to strangers who answered calls and start his pitch. When, as often happened, those strangers replied with a spew of invective against all insurance agents who took up their time, he had only to consult the appropriate line in his guidebook: "Yes, Mr. _____," he would say into the phone, "I understand how you feel, and I appreciate your frankness and point of view. But if you give me just a few minutes, I can show you . . ." More loud barking from the receiver, and the resonant clunk of the line going dead. There are more pleasant ways to earn a living than making cold calls.

While Moore's bosses want him to be a sales dynamo, you, his customer, also expect him to unearth opportunities for profitable investing that legions of full-time security analysts and money managers have somehow overlooked. He has his firm's research department to back him up in this. But by the time you hear of any idea from those analysts, you know that the institutional sales force has already spread the word to every big client in the country. No getting in on the ground floor for you. So nothing less than personalized service will do.

We also would like Moore to be multilingual in his financial expertise. He should speak the language not only of stocks, but of municipal bonds, options and futures, money markets, junk bonds, annuities, precious metals, and estate planning. All in all, it's a lot to expect of any mortal. Logic tells us that the population of brokers is pretty much a cross-section of people in general—a few doing an outstanding job, some very skillful and hardworking, many about average in the service they provide, some distinctly below average, and a few downright inept or corrupt. There's a lot of room there for disappointment. And we can't forget that, to excel on your behalf, a broker must somehow reconcile the conflict that often arises between what his employer expects from him—revenue—and what you the client want him to provide—time, enthusiasm, and wisdom, dispensed in liberal quantities at the lowest possible cost.

A general awareness of this conflict has helped give rise in the past decade or so to a new species known as the financial planner. On paper at least, financial planners are experts on matters of investing and money management who work for themselves or for independent firms. Thus they are supposedly beholden to no one and are in a better position than a broker to give impartial advice.

In practice, three types of financial planners have evolved, characterized by that most important of considerations, how they get paid. There is the *commission-only* planner, who operates somewhat like an independent insurance agent. Yes, this person, like a broker, relies on commission income for food in the refrigerator and a warm place to sleep. But since those commissions come from a variety of sources, he or she supposedly can offer a wide range of choices without prejudice. (Would such a planner have a natural human tendency to push the merchandise that paid the highest commissions? We'll leave that for you to judge.)

At the other end of the spectrum there is the *fee-only* financial planner. This individual avoids the problem of commissions altogether, relying for a livelihood solely on fees collected from clients. Under such an arrangement, a planner could talk to you just as enthusiastically about no-load mutual funds or dividend reinvestment plans as about high-commission items such as whole life insurance. In fact, this kind of planner may even be well qualified to advise you on ways to cut your investment costs. The trouble is, to make fee-only financial planning an attractive business to be in, the fees have to be pretty substantial. That skews the whole setup in favor of large investors over small. If you have just come into a million-dollar inheritance, a planner's fee of $5,000, $10,000, or even $20,000 might seem eminently worth the cost to get yourself organized. We can't speak from personal experience on this, but we've heard many times that money in large sums can be a frightening, as well as an exhilarating, thing to deal with. On the other hand, if you're trying to coax some growth out of a nest egg of $25,000 or $35,000, the idea of spending $5,000 to $10,000 for advice doesn't recommend itself.

The third type of planner is a hybrid: *part-commission, part-fee.* In the ideal, such a setup would blend the best of both categories. But it makes us suspicious. If we were hungry fellows just embarking on a career in financial planning, we'd choose this route. That way, we could collect from both sides.

We won't pretend that we're being "fair" on this whole subject. Some readers might well object that we don't know X, a financial planner who has helped them enormously at very reasonable cost. If that has been your experience, wonderful. Savor your good fortune, and send the planner more than a fruitcake at Christmastime. Still, it isn't easy to fit hiring a financial planner into any strategy we could think of that is truly no-cost/low-cost. If we are really serious about cutting the costs of managing money, we have to think in do-it-yourself terms.

In the event that you want more information about financial planners before deciding yea or nay, you can contact either of two trade organizations:

The Institute of Certified Financial Planners
3443 South Galena, Suite 190
Denver, CO 80231

*The International Association for
Financial Planning*
Two Concourse Parkway, Suite 800
Atlanta, GA 30328

A smaller organization which represents
strictly full-time, fee-only planners is:

*The National Association of
Personal Financial Advisors*
3726 Olentangy River Road
Columbus, OH 43214

A Farewell to
Full-Cost Investing

Now we've established our first priorities: whenever possible, we're going to act as our own brokers and use the commission savings to increase the amount of money we have available to invest. As our strategy becomes apparent to our amiable agent, Moore, and others of his occupation, we'll probably find them less eager to massage our egos and talk investments with us at social gatherings. Should we make financial choices that don't work out, we'll have to be emotionally limber enough to cry on our own shoulders. When we must use a broker, we'll seek out the cheapest one available that provides decent service. That's usually going to be a discount broker, the sort of operator who won't take us out for expense account lunches or play the devil's advocate when we adopt some investment strategy that is either just offbeat, as we hope, or crackbrained. It will be harder work operating on our own. Still, we won't have to go without any guidance whatsoever. Independent investment advisory services of many kinds (a sample list is at the end of this chapter) can provide us with information and ideas.

Besides, investing and managing money is a business, and we want to be businesslike about it. Part of being businesslike is to keep costs under firm control. The idea isn't to enrich ourselves and someone who has allied with us. It's simply to enrich ourselves. To pursue that goal, we'll have to resolve to see a lot less of Mr. Moore.

A Sampler of Investment Advisory Services

Hundreds of independent investment advisers offer their services to American investors. Their viewpoints range from what might be called mainstream to extremes of gloom and doom or political conservatism. It would be impossible, and probably undesirable as well, to list them all here. But we have compiled a representative roster of some of the largest and best known. If we have omitted a favorite of yours, be assured that it is not the result of any prejudice on our part.

Our listings do not include fees charged by these advisers, because many of them have complicated schedules of rates depending on the length of the subscription you buy and whether you also want their ancillary services such as personal consultations or access to telephone "hot-line" advice. In the spirit of no-cost/low-cost investing, you might want to inquire about cut-rate trial subscriptions to any advisory service that interests you.

The Value Line Investment Survey
711 Third Avenue
New York, NY 10017

Provides extensive statistical information, charts, analysis, rating system for about 1,700 stocks. Largest service in number of subscribers. Well known, respected. Weekly; each page on individual stocks updated every thirteen weeks on rotating basis.

The Outlook
Standard & Poor's Corp.
25 Broadway
New York, NY 10004
Commentary and recommendations aimed at conservative investors in stocks, bonds, mutual funds. Occasional feature: "Stocks to avoid." Weekly. Standard & Poor's also publishes monthly *Stock Guide* containing statistical information, which is used as a basic reference by many investors.

United & Babson Investment Report
210 Newbury Street
Boston, MA 02116
Wide range of investment advice, analysis and commentary. Weekly. Same publisher offers the separate *United Mutual Fund Selector.*

Market Logic
The Institute for Econometric Research
3471 North Federal Highway
Fort Lauderdale, FL 33306
Analyzes stock market, makes investment recommendations based on computer models and many indicators. Published twice a month. Publisher also offers: *New Issues,* on current and pending initial public stock offerings; *Mutual Fund Forecaster; Income and Safety;* and *The Insiders,* which covers dealings in stocks by top corporate executives and directors.

The Astute Investor
P.O. Box 988
Paoli, PA 19301
Commentary, investment advice by Robert Nurock.

Published seventeen times a year, "plus special bulletins as needed."

Investors Intelligence
30 Church Street
New Rochelle, NY 10801
Market commentary; tracks views of other advisory services as a basis for "contrary opinion."

The Professional Tape Reader
P.O. Box 2407
Hollywood, FL 33022
Publisher Stan Weinstein concentrates on technical analysis of the stock market, individual stocks, and options.

The Ground Floor
6 Deer Trail
Old Tappan, NJ 07675
Stock market letter focusing on small companies, new technology. Published twice a month. Publisher Yale Hirsch also offers monthly advisory letter called *Smart Money* and the annual *Stock Trader's Almanac*.

The Merrill Lynch Market Letter
Merrill Lynch Advisory Publications
North Tower (20th floor)
World Financial Center
New York, NY 10281–1215
Subscription-only advisory letter concentrating on stocks, applying both technical and fundamental analysis. Published twice a month.

The Zweig Forecast
P. O. Box 5345
New York, NY 10150
Market commentary, recommendations by analyst Martin Zweig.

Dessauer's Journal of Financial Markets
P.O. Box 1718
Orleans, MA 02653

Commentary by analyst John Dessauer on the economy, interest rates, stocks and bonds, precious metals. Published twice a month.

Dow Theory Letters
P.O. Box 1759
La Jolla, CA 92038
Commentary on investments, interest rates, precious metals by analyst Richard Russell.

The Elliott Wave Theorist
New Classic Library, Inc.
P.O. Box 1618-B
Gainesville, GA 30503
Advice on stocks, precious metals, interest rates from analyst Robert Prechter.

LaLoggia's Special Situation Report
P.O. Box 167
Rochester, NY 14601
Commentary, recommendations on stocks by analyst Charles LaLoggia. Published every three weeks.

Medical Technology Stock Letter
155 Montgomery Street
Suite 1401
San Francisco, CA 94104
Investment analysis specializing in biotechnology industry. Published every two weeks.

The Heim Investment Letter
P.O. Box 19435
Portland, OR 97219
Commentary, recommendations on stocks, precious metals. Published twice a month.

Deliberations
P.O. Box 182
Adelaide Street Station
Toronto, Ontario, Canada M5C 2J1
Technical analysis by Ian McAvity of stocks, bonds, currencies, and precious metals. Published twice a month.

Industry Forecast
Levy Economic Forecasts
Box 26
Chappaqua, NY 10514
Monthly commentary and forecasts on the economy
by economists David Levy and S. Jay Levy.

Brennan Reports
Valley Forge Office Colony
Suite 200
P.O. Box 882
Valley Forge, PA 19482
Monthly newsletter by William Brennan on the tax
aspects of investing and money management.

CHAPTER

2

DIVIDEND REINVESTMENT PLANS

Bargains, Bargains
and BARGAINS

To invest in the stock market at no cost means you would have to eliminate the stockbroker entirely, which may seem like pie in the sky. But there is in fact a way to do this. It is called a dividend reinvestment (DRI) plan, and it enables you to deal directly with the company you are investing in.

Such an end run around the broker's team, as you may well imagine, has been resisted by the brokerage community.

Many companies "don't allow individuals to invest directly in their dividend reinvestment plans," says Thomas E. O'Hara, chairman of the National Association of Investors Corp. (NAIC), "because the brokerage industry lobbies strongly against such plans." O'Hara's nonprofit organization provides investment education for individual investors and investment clubs.

Nevertheless, the DRI plan concept has gained a small foothold—half a dozen companies where it has eliminated the broker completely in buying shares—and also a large beachhead—about 1,000 companies where the broker is almost entirely removed as a middleman.

The DRI plan is for you if you are a patient, long-term investor. It is not for you if you are an in-and-out trader.

The fact is, it pays to be a patient, long-term investor. The rewards can be astounding. For instance, a $40 investment made today may not seem like much. But over a lifetime its growth can be almost unbelievable if you can pick the right company. To take a hypothetical example, let us say that Susan Smith was born in 1919 and that her proud grandparents immediately bought her one share of Coca-Cola, which was then worth $40. After reinvesting all her dividends at the end of each year, by January 1, 1987, Ms. Smith, now aged sixty-eight and retired, would be the owner of 10,204 shares worth $385,201. Quite a nice little retirement fund for $40.

This example assumes that no commission and no taxes were paid on the investment, two conditions that are most nearly met by (1) a commission-free DRI plan, and (2) a child with no other taxable income. Doting grandparents, take heed.

(All right, Grandpa, not every company is a Coca-Cola or an IBM. So pick ten small growth companies and invest $40 in each—easy enough to do through a DRI plan, as we will explain in detail further on—and for $400 one of them may hit the jackpot.)

Although hundreds of companies now offer DRI plans, the advantages of such plans evidently have not yet caught on very widely among investors. Manufacturers Hanover Trust Co., a big New York bank that administers the DRI plans for more than 100 corporations, says that only about 8% of shareholders participate in them.

The plans, it says, are generally more appealing to small investors.

However, companies that offer really outstanding bargains in their plans, such as discounted prices on reinvested dividends, and also on additional purchases of shares for cash, tend to have higher participation rates. Chesebrough-Pond's, for example, had 17,800 registered stockholders, and 6,700 of them, or nearly 40%, were in the DRI plan when Unilever U.S. Inc.—also recognizing a good investment, it seems—bought up the company in a tender offer at $72.50 a share in December 1986. This gave Chesebrough stockholders a nice profit since the company's stock had been trading in the $40 range only two months before the Unilever takeover.

Many companies are probably reluctant to advertise their DRI plans too extravagantly so as to avoid antagonizing the brokers who sell their shares. Nevertheless, the relative lack of interest in DRI plans is remarkable.

Consider the advantages:

1. Most of the plans give you the opportunity to open a stock market investment with only about $25 or $50.
2. A few plans do away with all your brokerage purchase costs entirely.
3. A very large number of plans eliminate all your brokerage purchase costs except for the commission on your initial investment, which might be as small as one share.
4. Many plans allow you to invest additional cash, as much as $60,000 a year in some cases, also without incurring any brokerage commissions.
5. A select minority go so far as to offer you a 3%, 5%, or even 10% discount on your reinvested dividends.
6. Some of these discounter plans do even more than that—they give you a similarly discounted price

for the additional cash investments you put into your plan.

Dollar-Cost Averaging

Over time, one major feature of the DRI plan is working relentlessly in your favor: dollar-cost averaging.

Your dividend is invested automatically every quarter at whatever the share price is on that date. You thus have a regular, methodical investment every three months. When the share price is high, your investment buys fewer shares, and when the price is low, it buys more. The end result of this is rather astonishing: over a period of time you end up paying less than the average price. Here is an example:

You invest $1,000 a year in the Roller Coaster Corporation. The price zooms and dives wildly between $5 and $20 over a four-year period. But, regardless of the price being high or low, you invest your fixed sum of $1,000 every January, come rain, sleet, or snow. This is how you make out:

	Share Price	Shares Bought for $1,000
Year 1	$10	100
Year 2	$ 5	200
Year 3	$20	50
Year 4	$10	100

Average price, $11.25.
Total shares bought, 450.

Your Roller Coaster stock swooped, climbed, and plunged, ending up at $10, exactly where it started. The average price of the stock over the whole period was

$11.25. You invested a total of $4,000 and ended up with 450 shares. Your average cost: $8.88 per share.

Magic, pure magic. One always finds this hard to believe.

How Dividend Reinvestment Plans Work

Most DRI plans do not issue stock certificates for your reinvested dividends, but they will do so if you request it, usually at a charge of $1 to $5. Statements are sent to you quarterly after the dividends are reinvested. Some companies purchase stock for the DRI plan on the stock market; others provide their own unissued new stock, in which case they have a specific procedure for establishing your purchase price. This might be the price on a specific date or an average stock market price over several days.

A large number of companies pay all the administration costs of their DRI plan. Some have a small charge of $2.50 per investment. Others assess a pro rata share of the brokerage commissions, but this usually comes to 1% or less—far below what an individual investor would pay on the same purchase. As an individual investor, your minimum brokerage commission would be about $30. Most plans also charge brokerage fees and transfer taxes when they sell your shares for you, but once again, this is at much lower cost than you would incur as an individual investor, because (1) the company usually bunches all the DRI investors' sales into one big order, and (2) it sometimes offsets these sales against purchases by other DRI plan investors.

If your DRI reinvestment does not quite cover a round number of shares, most DRI plans will make sure that all your money is working for you by assigning fractional shares to your credit.

You may already be a shareowner in the company

before joining its DRI plan. In this case, most plans give you the choice of keeping the share certificates in your possession or sending them in to be combined with your DRI holding.

A particularly attractive feature of some DRI plans, as noted above, is that they allow you to make additional cash investments on the same conditions as your dividends are reinvested. However, you are under no obligation to make regular cash payments or in fact any additional payments at all.

How to Do It

Now we get down to the nitty-gritty. You want to invest through DRI plans. How do you actually go about it? Which companies offer such plans? How can you contact them? In short, what do you do next?

We are assuming at this point that you don't own any stocks at all, that you have never had anything to do with the stock market, and that you need every detail explained every step of the way. If you are a more experienced and sophisticated investor than that, please bear with us and skip the more elementary explanations.

We are going to mention hundreds of companies in this chapter. They include some of the biggest and most prestigious corporations in the United States. Each company has its own particular dividend reinvestment plan, with its own details and peculiarities. To get all these things into a work of this size is impossible. It would require an encyclopedia. So we'll have to explain in detail how a few representative DRI plans work and then tell you how to contact the other companies yourself. If you are interested in investing in any of them, you might write to the company in question directly. Ask for the company's latest yearly report to stockholders, its latest quarterly report, and the prospectus of its dividend reinvestment plan. The yearly report will give you an overall idea of the company's general business and condition; the quarterly report will tell you how it has been doing in the past few months. And then, if you like what you see, you can look into the DRI plan.

To establish some kind of order, let's organize our list of available companies on the basis of what we might call the hassle factor.

A Few Easy Ones

To begin with, here are a few companies that will give you an absolute minimum of fuss and bother when you decide to initiate a DRI plan with them. These are companies where you do not have to deal with a broker at all from beginning to end. You simply write the company directly, ask for its DRI plan prospectus, fill out the application form, and send it back to the company with your first check, which could be as small as $25.

These companies include Citicorp, Control Data Corp., W.R. Grace & Co., Great Northern Nekoosa Corp., and Johnson Controls. Citicorp is the biggest commercial bank in the world; Control Data is into computers and financing; Grace has worldwide operations in chemicals, energy, and retailing; Great Northern Nekoosa makes paper and paper products; and Johnson Controls manufactures building controls, auto batteries, and processing systems.

If you invested in these five companies, you would have your investments spread out over a wide diversity of business activities, a major safety feature for prudent investors.

Now, how much money do you need? Citicorp requires an initial investment of $250, Control Data $50, Grace $50, Nekoosa $25, and Johnson Controls $50. So you could set up the whole thing for $425 altogether. It would be only $135 if you exclude Citicorp. And not a penny in commissions to anyone in any case.

Or, if you are a real big-shot investor, let's take a look at the maximum amount you could invest. Citicorp will allow you to put in $48,000 per year, Control Data $36,000, Grace $60,000, Nekoosa $25,000, and Johnson Controls $60,000. Total $229,000 in the first year—still without a cent in commissions—and another commission-free $229,000 for any subsequent year if you should happen to win the lottery.

A Couple of Sample Plans

Let's say you want to start out small—real small—while you feel your way ahead and make up your mind whether this DRI business is really for you. This is how the picture looks as this book is written—the outlook may be different by the time you read it. Citicorp's $250 minimum seems rather rich for our budget. Control Data is not doing too well and has skipped recent dividends, so let's skip that one. Nekoosa appears to be pretty highly specialized and vulnerable to the ups and downs of the paper industry. Not for now, Nekoosa. That leaves us with W.R. Grace, which has worldwide operations in a number of industries, and Johnson Controls, a highly regarded American technology company. With these two investments, if the U.S. economy does badly and Johnson Controls slips with it, we still have Grace and its global activities as insurance against a U.S. recession.

So we start with Grace. First, write to W.R. Grace & Co., Dividend Reinvestment and Stock Purchase Plan, 1114 Avenue of the Americas, New York, NY 10109. You will get back a package that includes the company's latest yearly report, a brochure explaining the DRI plan, and an application form that looks like Exhibit 2-1.

W. R. Grace & Co.   Authorization for Dividend Reinvestment and Common Stock Purchase Plan

I hereby authorize Marine Midland Bank, N.A. as my agent, subject to the Plan Terms and Conditions, to apply any cash dividend and/or cash payment received by it on my behalf to the purchase of shares of Grace Common Stock, as follows (check one box at right):

☐ 1. **Full Dividend Reinvestment (For Record Shareholders Only)**
I wish to reinvest dividends on all shares registered in my name. I may also make supplemental cash payments at my discretion.

☐ 2. **Partial Dividend Reinvestment (For Record Shareholders Only)**
I wish to have dividends reinvested on _____ (fill in number) shares registered in my name. I may also make supplemental cash payments at my discretion.

☐ 3. **Cash Payments**
I wish to make cash payments. Enclosed is my check or money order **payable to W. R. Grace & Co.** for $_____ ($.50 minimum) as my initial cash payment.

Signature (1) _____

Signature (2) _____

PLEASE COMPLETE REVERSE SIDE OF CARD

9

Please **print** or **type** information exactly as shown on your dividend check, if applicable. If not currently a shareholder, please provide the information to open your Plan account. Be sure to include your shareholder account number if you are presently a Participant.

Name (1)

Name (2)

Street Address

City   State   Zip Code

Social Security Number   Shareholder Account Number (if applicable)

PLEASE COMPLETE REVERSE SIDE OF CARD

9

Exhibit 2-1

The question now is whether you want to fill this thing out and send in your $50, which is all there is to opening a Grace DRI plan.

Leafing through the company's yearly report, you learn that Grace does $4 billion worth of business worldwide in chemicals, coal, and fertilizer; in Hungry Tiger, El Torito, and Taco Villa restaurants; in Herman's Sporting Goods, Robinson Jewelers, and other businesses in various fields. Earnings per share have been declining for the past four years from $6.10 to $2.94, but the chairman is optimistic about the future and the dividend paid out has been steady at $2.80 per share for the past four years. You look up the latest quote for W.R. Grace in your local newspaper or the *Wall Street Journal* and find it closed at 50¾ ($50.75). The dividend yield is thus 5.5%.

There is a whole lot of other information in the yearly report, and on the basis of it all you may decide to go ahead and invest in the company. Or you may decide that you need some additional information from an outside impartial source. In that case you might consult *Standard & Poor's Stock Guide*. This little booklet comes out monthly and is an astonishingly compact source of up-to-date statistical data on several thousand companies. A yearly subscription costs $88. Write to Standard & Poor's Corp., 25 Broadway, P.O. Box 992, New York, NY 10275. A single monthly copy (any month) may be obtained for $10 from Standard & Poor's Parts Department, 345 Hudson Street, New York, NY 10014. Or better still—to keep the faith with the no-cost/low-cost philosophy of this book—you may be able to get a free look at the *Stock Guide* in the business section of your local public library.

In view of Grace's declining earnings, let's check the *Stock Guide*. We find that Grace has paid a cash dividend every single year since 1934, which looks reassuring. The stock's price has ranged from a high of 60¾ to a low of 35½ in the last three years, so the current price of about $50 is toward the high end of the range. You will note that Standard & Poor's has a computerized system for rating the quality of the company stocks listed. The system is based mainly on the stability and growth of company earnings and dividends over the years. The ratings range from A+, the highest, to D, which means a company in bankruptcy proceedings. In the *Stock Guide* we see that Grace gets a B+, just average.

You decide to fill out the application form and send in your $50.

Now turn to the Grace brochure on its DRI plan. You should get your payment in before the sixth of the month. Otherwise it will be held over until the following month. On a $50 investment this is not going to make much difference, but it will if you invest substantial amounts because Grace says that no interest is paid on the funds awaiting investment. On the tenth of each month Grace makes the stock purchase for you and for all other DRI investors. They are all combined in one big purchase order to lower commission rates—not that this affects you at all since Grace, not you, pays all the transaction costs.

You should note here that you will just have to take your chance on whatever the stock price is on the purchase date. You cannot specify the maximum price you are willing to pay, as you might perhaps choose to do when purchasing through a broker.

Once your investment is in, you will get a confirmation for all the shares or fractional shares that you have acquired with your $50. Every three months after that, your DRI plan will credit you with the company's quarterly dividend, which will be reinvested for you without any commission being charged.

The fact is, however, that this dividend reinvestment is probably the least valuable part of the Grace DRI plan. The important thing is that as a member of the plan you are now entitled to make further monthly investments of $50 to $5,000, all of them without paying a cent in commissions. This means that from here on out you can build up your investment for years and years without paying any commissions at all. In addition, you are under no obligation. You add to your investments purely at your own convenience.

Grace will hold your shares in the DRI plan account, but if you want the certificates delivered to you, the company will do that too at no charge and continue the DRI plan for you as before. When you want to sell your shares in the DRI plan, you merely inform Grace, which will charge you $1 plus brokerage commissions and any transfer tax. The commissions will be considerably lower than you would incur in selling the equivalent amount of shares yourself through a broker because Grace reduces commissions by offsetting the sales against DRI purchases that day and combining the remaining shares to be sold into one big lot. When the time comes to end your participation in the Grace DRI plan, you can ask Grace either to send your shares to you or pay you off in cash.

Our second company, Johnson Controls, which incidentally gets an A rating from Standard & Poor's (just one step below the top-rated A+), has an equally simple form to fill out (Exhibit 2-2).

The address of Johnson Controls is 5757 N. Green Bay Avenue, P.O. Box 591, Milwaukee, WI 53201. You can invest $50 to $15,000 initially, and then amounts within the same range quarterly—not to exceed $15,000 per quarter.

Meanwhile you decide that perhaps the Citicorp dividend reinvestment plan is too tempting a deal to pass by after all. Citicorp claims to be the largest and most profitable investor-owned financial services company in the world. It does in fact get Standard & Poor's top A+ rating. In addition to its thousands of corporate customers, it does business with 16.6 million households in the United States and another 6.2 million abroad. Citicorp is a truly global enterprise, with 3,000 offices around the world in more than ninety countries. It has 80,000 employees. What is more to the point for our purpose, Citicorp has paid uninterrupted dividends every year since 1813, and dividends have grown by 10% every year for the past decade. The future, however, is not necessarily a prolongation of past trends. Citicorp has billions of dollars out in loans to financially shaky countries such as Mexico, Brazil, and Argentina, and could run into serious financial difficulties if they should default. It is also planning to expand into insurance and financial information, two fields in which it may possibly not be as successful as it has been in banking in the past two centuries.

Still, it seems a good bet for $250. The Citicorp stock purchase and dividend reinvestment plan is open to anyone who is willing to invest at least $250 in the company. If you make any subsequent investments they must also be at least $250—and can be as high as $60,000 a year if you have that kind of money.

Whatever amount you invest, you pay no commissions when buying. Whenever you decide to sell, you pay a $5 administrative charge and a stock withdrawal charge of 1%. Citicorp notes that if you invested, say, $3,000 in Citicorp stock through a broker you would pay about $70 in commissions to a full-service broker (plus another $70 when you sold). A discount broker would charge you $35 to $55 to buy. You would thus spend from $70 to $140 in brokerage commissions to buy and sell. The DRI plan can thus save you more than 3.5% commissions on a $3,000 purchase and sale—and a much, much higher percentage on a $250 purchase—which would in fact be so prohibitive in cost that you would be crazy to make it at all through a broker.

Citibank N.A., the main banking arm of Citicorp, holds all your shares in safekeeping for you, or you can request delivery of your certificates to you at no charge. You can sell part of your shares at any time and keep your DRI plan open with the remainder, provided at least one full share remains in your account. The money you

AUTHORIZATION FORM

JOHNSON CONTROLS AUTOMATIC DIVIDEND REINVESTMENT AND COMMON STOCK PURCHASE PLAN

CHECK ONE BOX ONLY.

☐ 1. Full Dividend Reinvestment.
   I wish to reinvest dividends on all shares registered in my name.

☐ 2. Partial Dividend Reinvestment.
   I wish to have dividends reinvested on _____ (enter number) Common/Preferred (circle one) shares registered in my name.

☐ 3. Supplemental Cash – For Shareholders Only
   Enclosed is my check or money order in the amount of
   $ _____ ($50 minimum) to purchase shares of Common Stock.

☐ 4. Initial Cash Only – For Non-Shareholders Only
   Enclosed is my check or money order in the amount of
   $ _____ ($50 minimum) as my initial cash investment.
   Dividends on shares acquired through the Plan and held in my Plan account will be fully reinvested.

I hereby authorize First Wisconsin Trust Company as my agent, subject to the Description of the Plan, to apply an initial investment, cash dividend and/or supplemental cash investment received by it on my behalf to the purchase of shares of Johnson Controls Common Stock. **Sign below exactly as name appears on reverse side.**

_____ *

_____ *

Date

* Under penalties of perjury, I certify (1) that the number shown on the reverse of this form is my correct Taxpayer Identification Number and (2) that I am not subject to backup withholding.

AUTHORIZATION FORM

Shareholders Only: If a pre-printed label is affixed below, verify accuracy and make any needed changes.
Non-Shareholders Only: Please print or type information exactly as you wish to register your account. You may wish to consult legal counsel for the appropriate type of ownership (e.g. tenants in common; tenants by entireties; etc.)

Name (1)

Name (2)

Street Address

City   State/Country   Zip Code

Social Security Number (1)   Social Security Number (2)

I am a U.S. citizen ☐ Yes ☐ No

BE SURE TO COMPLETE BOTH SIDES OF FORM.
MAIL TO FIRST WISCONSIN TRUST COMPANY, P.O. BOX 2054, MILWAUKEE, WI 53201

Exhibit 2-2
Johnson Controls DRI Application Form

send in for investment must be received by Citicorp at least thirty days prior to the four quarterly investment dates in the year. This means getting your money in just before January 10, April 10, July 10, or October 10. As no interest is paid on funds awaiting investment, it pays not to miss one of these deadlines.

The address is Citicorp, Dividend Reinvestment Plan, 111 Wall Street, Sort 5710, New York, NY 10043.

The addresses of the other two companies, in case you want to get to them later, are: Control Data, Dividend Reinvestment Plan, P.O. Box 0, Minneapolis, MN 55440; Great Northern Nekoosa Corp., Dividend Reinvestment Plan, P.O. Box 9309, Stamford, CT 06904.

Another Ten Companies— With a Slight Catch

To these five companies we will now add another ten which also allow you to initiate a DRI plan by applying directly to the company without going through a broker—provided you meet certain conditions.

The first one is an investment for bowlers, of all things. American Recreation Centers Inc., of Sacramento, California, which has a chain of bowling centers, will let you join its DRI plan if you are (1) already a stockholder, or (2) "an adult League bowler of the company," which is to say a patron of its bowling lanes. You can invest $50 to $500 initially, and after that $10 to $500 a month if you feel like it. The address is 9261 Folsom Blvd., Bldg. 300, P.O. Box 60729, Sacramento, CA 95860. Investors who own 300 shares or more, says company president Robert Feuchter, get an extra bonus—"unlimited open [casual] bowling" at the company's 1,074 bowling lanes.

And, if you are tired of your local utility company making money off you in gas and electric bills, here is your chance to make money out of your utility company.

If you happen to live in the right location, the following nine utilities have DRI plans only for their customers that you can join by applying to the company directly rather than buying stock through a broker:

1. Central Hudson Gas & Electric Corp., Pough-keepsie, New York.
2. Cleveland Electric Illuminating Co., Cleveland, Ohio.
3. Dominion Resources Inc., Richmond, Virginia.
4. Duke Power Co., Charlotte, North Carolina.
5. Montana Power Co., Butte, Montana.
6. Portland General Electric Co., Portland, Oregon.
7. Puget Sound Power & Light Co., Bellevue, Washington.
8. San Diego Gas & Electric Co., San Diego, California.
9. Union Electric Co., St. Louis, Missouri.

An IRA Plan

And let us not forget to add one oddball plan if you are looking for an IRA investment and happen to like utilities. Pacificorp, based in Portland, Oregon, has a DRI plan that it will not let you join unless you are already a shareholder in the company. It waives that requirement, however, if you plan to open an Individual Retirement Account investing exclusively in Pacificorp stock. You pay a $5 account opening fee and a yearly $20 maintenance fee, but no brokerage commissions. The minimum investment is $50 and the maximum is the standard $2,000 yearly limit for all IRA plans. Pacificorp, incidentally, gets an A rating from Standard & Poor's and combines coal, gold, and silver mining with its utility business. This is an intriguing combination, apparently suited to survival under all economic conditions: utilities generally do well when inflation and interest rates are low, while coal, gold, and silver mining tend to do well when inflation and interest rates are high. The address is Pacificorp, Power IRA Program, Room 1000, 851 S.W. Sixth Ave., Portland, OR 97204.

The Wave of the Future

This little beachhead of a dozen or so companies where you no longer need a broker to buy or sell stock deserves some further exploration, for it may well be the wave of the future in the stock market as companies and individual investors reach out to each other for salvation—the companies to escape the clutches of huge institutional investors that sometimes wreak havoc on their stock prices and corporate fortunes, and the individual investors to avoid the high expense of brokerage commissions.

There have been dividend reinvestment plans chugging routinely along for many years now, but they were open only to investors who were already stockholders. The company that opened up the game to the general public—to anyone at all with $50 to invest—was Control Data. This innovation may have started a whole new investment era.

The Minneapolis-based computer and financial services company launched its DRI plan in January 1981, but it appeared unheralded and uncelebrated. The company was warned not to publicize or advertise the plan. "Our understanding with the SEC was that there would be no aggressive advertising," said Burton Traub, vice-president for investor relations. Nevertheless the company quickly picked up about 2,000 new stockholders who heard of the plan by word of mouth, and participation spread rapidly from there on.

A major instigator of the Control Data DRI plan was William E. Chatlos, a financial expert of an original turn of mind who now runs his own consulting firm, Chatlos

& Co., Inc., in North Caldwell, New Jersey. Chatlos is eloquent and outspoken about what he sees as a major corporate problem of the 1980s: the failure to treat investors fairly.

In the 1960s, he says, "the infuriating arrogance of Wall Street drove individuals out of the marketplace. In 1967 and 1968 the back offices in Wall Street got so botched up it sometimes took nine months to get a stock certificate from the transfer agent to the investor. Wall Street's reaction to this was to close down every Wednesday. They had the only game in town, so they just slowed down the game. Shareholders lost money, they were lied to, cheated, given bad service and bad advice. They took a walk and left the market."

In the 1970s the big financial institutions swarmed all over Wall Street and took over the stock market, accounting for the bulk of trading volume. "They brought their own ground rules," says Chatlos, "which ended up with them owning Wall Street as they do today."

"The institutions," said Chatlos, "wound up trading in what came to be known as the nifty-fifty top companies. Well over 95% of the stocks from then on had neither individuals nor institutions following them to any great degree, and became targets of one corporate takeover after another."

About the only time a shareholder might get a fair price, according to Chatlos, is when his company becomes the target of a takeover attempt.

"From that point on," he says, "company managements have been faced with the problem that they're worth more dead than alive. This is going to be the major problem of the 1980s, because they will not be able to hide anymore."

The big institutions—banks, mutual funds, pension funds, and others—"have an average stock holding period of only nine months," Chatlos observes. "They have no loyalty to the company they invest in. These gorillas in white spats own the market at present and have the money. Do you know of any companies that really like institutional ownership? The fact is, companies are under more and more jeopardy from big institutions. One day they are going to wake up and find the solution."

The solution, according to Chatlos, is the dividend reinvestment plan to attract a broad, solid, stable base of small individual investors.

James Stier, director of shareholder relations at W.R. Grace & Co., which quickly followed Control Data's lead in setting up a DRI plan open to the general public, agrees with Chatlos on this point. "The bedrock of any public corporation," says Stier, "is to be owned by as many individuals as you can possibly attract. The big institutions are fickle. They have no allegiance to the company. It's purely dollars and cents to them. Also, there's no hope that a mutual fund will go out and patronize your restaurants or buy your products. With individual shareholders that possibility exists, and strongly so. If the company is in difficulty individual shareholders are not necessarily going to sell the stock. If there's a proxy fight they may support the management."

Stier points out two facts: first, 41% of Grace stockholders—13,000 of them—are now in the company's DRI plan and the percentage is climbing. Second, Grace stock rose in price in recent years despite declining earnings, indicating growing stockholder appreciation of the company's value.

When Control Data first took its plan to the SEC for approval, Chatlos recalls, "there was a lot of mumbling and grumbling from the brokers. They said, you'll put us out of business. I said, you brokers have done nothing for the individual investor. Even your Monthly Investment Plan with which you tried to attract the small investor is dead because you couldn't sell it. All we have done is bring up an idea that you yourselves threw away. We are not taking anything from you. We are taking accounts you don't even want."

"In arguing with the SEC," Chatlos remembers, "I

said just try buying two or three shares of General Motors and see what commission you have to pay. I asked, why is the SEC discriminating against small investors? Let everybody become a shareholder through a DRI plan, but just think what reception I'm going to get from a broker when I want to buy one share and the broker knows I'm starting a DRI plan and will have no further need of him.

"The SEC staffer said, 'Fine but I don't want anyone coming in on anything less than full disclosure.' I said, 'You can have all the disclosure you want, but give shareholders direct access.' And so the Control Data plan was approved." But the company was warned about "agressive advertising."

Chatlos foresees great prospects for open-access DRI plans. "The future of this is still ahead of us," he says. "Suppose a maker of breakfast cereals puts a line on all its corn flakes packages saying: 'This company has a stock purchase and dividend reinvestment plan; write for details.' The customer would then get the plan prospectus and might become an investor. This is a marketing tool with huge possibilities and at minimal cost. It could create market loyalty to brands from shareholders and it would increase sales. Ford stockholders don't usually buy GM cars."

Whatever the future may hold, however, there are so far only a handful of DRI direct-access plans available, and if you want to invest in the hundreds of traditional DRI plans that are open only to company stockholders you will have to find some way of becoming a stockholder without paying the initial brokerage commissions.

NAIC Plans

We now come to another two dozen companies you can buy without using a broker even though their DRI plans normally require initial purchase through a broker. The way around this requirement is through the National Association of Investors Corp., a nonprofit organization dedicated to assisting individual investors and investment clubs. These companies are:

Aetna Life & Casualty
American Family Corp.
Ashland Oil
Armco Inc.
Avery International
Brown Forman Inc.
Central Maine Power Co.
Dana Corp.
Day International
The Walt Disney Company
Dow Chemical Co.
Federal-Mogul Corp.
Foxboro Co.
General Signal Corp.
Gerber Products Co.
W.R. Grace & Co.
Hannaford Bros. Co.
Harsco Corp.
Hospital Corp. of America
Iowa Resources Inc.
Kellogg Company
McDonald's Corp.
NBD Bancorp.
Primark Corp.
Quaker Oats Co.
Quanex Corp.
RPM Inc.
St. Paul Companies Inc.

The NAIC has joined the DRI plans of the above companies. As a member of the NAIC (the cost of membership is $30), you can join any or all of these DRI plans by filling in the NAIC form reproduced in Exhibit 2-3, writing out a check for the amount of the investments you are planning to make, and mailing to NAIC, 1515 East Eleven Mile Road, Royal Oak, MI 48067.

NAIC will forward your money for investment to the companies you select. Once your first purchase has been made, your own account will be set up and you send future payments directly to the corporation's DRI plan agent. To cover setup and handling costs, you pay NAIC a onetime charge of $5 for each stock you wish to buy. Your other costs depend on the company whose stock you choose to invest in.

NAIC points out that you can join the DRI plans of these companies without going through NAIC, "but our way is quicker and less costly. On your own, you would go to your broker and order one or more shares; you would contact the corporation for an application to enter its DRI plan. Then you would send your application and money to the corporation's agent and begin the plan. The advantage of using NAIC is that NAIC has already bought stock and is in the company's plan. You can start immediately, and you don't bear the cost of buying your own share at brokerage rates or suffer the delay of completing the purchase, waiting for the delivery of the share certificate, receiving your own application, and then entering the plan on your own."

NAIC chairman Thomas E. O'Hara observes that the organization has been in business for thirty-six years attempting to teach individuals sound investment procedures. He notes that the NAIC low-cost investment plan "permits an individual to start by investing just enough to buy one share of stock. Regular additions can then be made with as little as $10 per quarter." Thus "individuals can invest small amounts, invest on an installment basis, and do so at practically no cost."

Among the companies you can buy through NAIC, the following appear to be outstanding: Aetna and Hospital Corp. of America offer you a 5% discount, but on

How to start your own regular investment plan

If you want to start building a security account using NAIC's new plan, just fill in the coupon below.

Mark it to show whether you want to invest in one or more companies. The Corporate brief accompanying this folder lists the companies whose plan NAIC has joined and can make available to you. Choose from this list of companies.

The sooner you start, the quicker you'll acquire your own security account. Why not today?

NATIONAL ASSOCIATION
OF INVESTORS CORPORATION

INVESTMENT EDUCATION
SINCE 1951

Send check to: NAIC ESCROW ACCOUNT
1515 East Eleven Mile Road
Royal Oak, Michigan 48067

Please enroll me in your new Regular Investment Program

Start my Investment with Amount Shown Below.

Name(s) of Company I Want to Invest in

Add $10 to the price of one share as quoted in your daily paper to cover price fluctuations and round to even dollars. Larger investments can be made when you own account is established.

One Time Set-up charge of $5 per Company

Totals a & b (Add Amounts)

1. _____ (a) $. _____ (b) $ _____ $ _____

2. _____ (a) $ _____ (b) $ _____ $ _____

3. _____ (a) $ _____ (b) $ _____ $ _____

When your request is received by NAIC, you will be mailed an application form and a detailed description of the plan for the company (or companies) you wish to invest in. When your card is returned to NAIC and your first deposit has been invested, your account will be transferred directly into your own name and you will receive instructions on where to send future investments.

You must be a member of NAIC to participate in this program. Please show your NAIC number here: _____. (Give the first five digits in back of your name on your Better Investing address label.)

If you are not now a member, you can join by checking this box ☐ *and adding $30.00 to your check.* . . . . $ _____

As an individual joining NAIC, you join tens of thousands building a better America through investing, you will receive a copy of the valued "Investors Manual" the textbook for learn-by-doing investing; a one year's subscription to Better Investing Magazine, America's only magazine devoted to Investment Education with dozens of ideas to help you be a more profitable investor; and all the other privileges of NAIC membership.

SEND CHECK FOR TOTAL OF ALL ABOVE ITEMS TO: NAIC ESCROW ACCOUNT $ _____

Signed _____ Soc. Sec. No. _____

Address _____

City, State, Zip _____

CONGRATULATIONS, you've taken your First Step in a Regular Investment Plan to build a holding of securities. Plan to invest regularly.

Individuals and Investment Club members have been working to build a better America through Better Investing since 1951.

Exhibit 2-3
NAIC Form

reinvested dividends only, not on additional investments. Avery International, Hospital Corp. of America, Kellogg Co., McDonald's, and Quaker Oats are all top-notch companies rated A+ by Standard & Poor's. This is the highest possible rating, shared by less than 200 other American corporations.

NAIC can provide you with brief reports on each of the companies included in its low-cost investment program. The charge is $3 for each five reports requested.

NAIC stresses three points for a really successful investment program:

1. Invest a set sum of money regularly over a long period of time.
2. Reinvest your dividends.
3. Invest in companies that give promise of being more valuable organizations in five years.

"Following these principles," says NAIC, "one of our members invested at the rate of $20 a month in a number of different companies. After thirty-seven years, he had invested $11,280 in monthly payments. His reinvested earnings and appreciation of the securities he had purchased allowed him to spend $35,000 from his account and still have securities left worth $71,000."

Another 300 Companies
Available Without a Broker

So far we have about forty companies you can buy without paying a broker. Let us now add a further 300 or so to this list.

The Moneypaper (2 Madison Ave., Larchmont, NY 10538), a monthly publication on money matters and personal finance, offers a similar service to that provided by NAIC. *Moneypaper* has a list of about 300 stocks with DRI plans where you can bypass brokers and make the initial purchase of one share through *Moneypaper*. The cost is a $54 yearly subscription to *Moneypaper* and a $15 service fee for each stock you buy. After your initial one-share investment, you make all further payments commission-free directly to the company's DRI plan. You thus have a flat $15 purchase fee on each stock and no further brokerage purchase costs from there on, no matter how many shares you subsequently buy.

This is the way it works. *Moneypaper* publishes a list of a dozen to two dozen stocks in each monthly issue, usually grouped by category, such as twelve stocks that have increased their dividends every year for the past ten years (a major point to consider in a dividend reinvestment plan), or fifteen growth stocks (another major consideration for the long-term DRI plan investor).

If any of these companies looks like a good buy to you, look up the latest stock market quote in your daily newspaper, add $7 to cover any possible price fluctuations (the $7 is refundable), add a $15 service fee, and send the total amount to *Moneypaper*, which will buy you one share to set up your own DRI plan. Once that is established, you can then make additional payments whenever you wish directly to the DRI company involved, with no middleman's fees or commissions.

To make all this quite clear, Exhibit 2-4 shows a listing of one *Moneypaper* selection of stocks and the application form you would have to fill in. These are twenty-one companies that have raised their dividends every year for at least the past ten years. Most of them are rated A to A+ by Standard & Poor's.

Duane Frederic, who teaches finance at Notre Dame College in South Euclid, Ohio, is the man who puts these lists together for *Moneypaper*. He says many *Moneypaper* subscribers order nine stocks every month from these lists. He himself owns stock in more than 350 companies with dividend reinvestment plans. Frederic writes a monthly investment column in *The Moneypaper* and maintains an updated list of about 1,000 companies with

☐ I want to get invested in the DRP of the following stocks:

Name of Stock	div up	recent $	purchase date
Waste Management (WMX/A)	42.6%	57	1st bus day
McDonald's Corporation (MCD/A+)	41.5	63	5th bus day
RPM, Inc. (RPMOW/A−)	36.3	20	last bus day
National Medical Enterprises (NME/A)	32.0	24	15th
EG&G, Inc. (EGG/A)	29.2	29	1st
Amer. Medical International (AMI/A−)	28.2	15	1st
Tracor, Inc. (TRR/A)	26.7	18	1st
Browning-Ferris Industries (BFI/A+)	25.7	46	5th
Hospital Corp. of America (HCA/A+)	24.9	31	1st
Philip Morris Companies (MO/A+)	23.5	73	10th
Church's Fried Chicken (CHU/B+)	22.3	12	5th
Abbott Laboratories (ABT/A+)	22.2	48	2/15/87
General Cinema (GCN/A+)	22.0	45	1/30/87
Dean Foods (DF/A+)	21.8	29	3/15/87
Baxter Travenol Laboratories (BAX/A)	21.7	20	1st
H.J. Heinz (HNZ/A+)	19.4	42	10th
G. Heileman Brewing (GHB/A+)	18.9	24	1st
Mortgage & Realty Trust (MRT/NR)	18.1	23	2/15/87
AMP (AMP/A)	18.0	37	1st
Dayton-Hudson Corporation (DH/A+)	17.7	43	10th
NCR (NCR/A)	17.6	46	1/30/87

Print subscriber's name, address and zip code above

(Optional) Phone #/time to call

Name of Stock (from those offered)	Price plus $7 refundable*	Service fee (not refundable)	Cost
1.	$ _____	+ $7	+ $15	= $
2.	$ _____	+ $7	+ $15	= $
3.	$ _____	+ $7	+ $15	= $
4.	$ _____	+ $7	+ $15	= $
5.	$ _____	+ $7	+ $15	= $
6.	$ _____	+ $7	+ $15	= $
7.	$ _____	+ $7	+ $15	= $
8.	$ _____	+ $7	+ $15	= $
9.	$ _____	+ $7	+ $15	= $

If you are not a subscriber to THE MONEYPAPER check this box ☐ and add $54 for a year's subscription. Include your complete mailing address. $ _____

Total $ _____

Print name(s) exactly as you want stock registered

Social Security or Taxpayer Identification #
Note: Under current tax law, you must supply valid taxpayer ID or be subject to 20% withholding on dividends.

Proper stock registration is full first name, middle initial (preferred) or middle name, and last name. On joint tenancy accounts, provide the SS # for the first person named. On custodian accounts for minors, provide full name for both custodian and child; supply SS # for child only.

*See box on page 9 for additional explanation

Exhibit 2-4
Typical Moneypaper *Stock Selection and DRI*
Application Form (January 1987 Issue)

dividend reinvestment plans. The list is available from *The Moneypaper* for $15.

Frederic comments: "I recommend having at least ten stocks in your portfolio. It is advisable to further minimize risk by diversifying in terms of industry groups as well. It is easy to afford a portfolio of ten or more stocks, since you need only one share to participate in any of these stocks' DRI plans. Once you are enrolled, you may send in optional investments of at least $25 to a maximum of $5,000 per quarter to buy more shares. If you do this, you'll be pleasantly surprised how quickly your holdings will increase."

Moneypaper, incidentally, provides all kinds of other information on such topics as how to buy ocean-cruise tickets at half-price and other money-saving ideas.

Person to Person

One further possibility is to buy one or more shares from a stockholder of the company you are interested in if you happen to know any such or can contact one. However this is rather a nuisance as it involves getting signature guarantees. Once you have your seller lined up, agree on a price—such as the closing price on the day you make the deal—and send him your check for that amount, no commissions for either of you. If the seller happens to have a certificate for one share (or ten or however many you are buying) he then endorses the certificate over to you as per the instructions on the back. If the seller does not have a certificate for the proper number of shares you agreed on, then he has to write to the company's DRI plan agent instructing the agent to transfer X number of shares to your name and stating that you want to join the plan. The seller's signature on this letter—or on the shares transferred, if they change hands directly between you—must be guaranteed by a commercial banker or a stock brokerage firm. Some transfer agents perform their service free; others charge as much as $5. The whole process can take up to two months.

So You Pay a Commission, but on One Share Only

We are now up to about 350 companies you can buy without any assistance at all from your friendly broker. There are still about 700 more that you can buy through DRI plans. But on these you are going to be nicked, at least on the initial purchase, for a broker's commission.

This need not be more than a fleabite, however, compared with your usual dealings with a broker. Ownership of only one share is usually all that is required to open a DRI plan with most companies offering them. If you already have a brokerage account, simply order your broker to buy one share for you.

You may feel embarrassed about this. You may feel like a piker. Your broker may laugh at you. He may perhaps refuse to take the order. Tell him that if he doesn't give you the service you want you will close your account; then close it. And if he is an expensive full-service broker, then move your account to a discount broker.

In any case, here is one more important point. Tell your broker the share is to be registered in your name, not in "street name." In "street name" means that it is registered on the company's books in the name of the brokerage house. You are the owner, but your name does not figure on the company's records. This kind of registration has certain benefits if you are an active trader because it facilitates frequent buying and selling without entangling you in mailing share certificates back and forth.

But in this case it is essential that you avoid this procedure because most companies offering DRI plans will not let you enroll unless you are a stockholder of record. They want your name on their books.

Once you have your share delivered to you, contact the company and ask it for its DRI plan prospectus. In some cases you may keep the certificate in your possession. In others you may turn it in to the company's plan administrator, which may be the company itself or a bank that specializes in this kind of business. What the procedure is depends on each individual plan.

At the end of this chapter we name several hundred companies listed on the New York Stock Exchange that offer dividend reinvestment plans, another sixty or so companies quoted on the American Stock Exchange, and more than one hundred more traded on the over-the-counter market.

However, some of these plans are more attractive than others. Before you go browsing through these three lists looking for possible investments, let us highlight for you some of the company plans that have really outstanding features.

Shares at a Discount

First of all, how about buying shares at a discount? Yes, there actually are some companies that are so eager to have you as a stockholder that they will offer you a discount of as much as 10% off the going market price on the shares you buy with your reinvested dividends. Not only that, but a select few will even allow you to make additional investments for cash, also at a discount of up to 10%. In most cases the discount is 5%, in some cases 3%.

If you are of a suspicious turn of mind you might think that only shaky, flaky, dubious companies teetering on the edge of bankruptcy and desperate for new investors would offer you this kind of deal. Indeed there may be such cases. It pays to investigate every time.

Nevertheless, you will find solid, reputable, true-blue corporations among the discounters.

Here, for instance, is Norstar Bancorp, a New York State bank that has paid dividends since 1804. Or First of America Bank Corp., a Michigan bank holding company that has not skipped a dividend since 1864. Or First Union Corp., a North Carolina bank holding company that has not missed a dividend since 1914. Or Multibank Financial Corp., a Massachusetts banking company that has paid out dividends without interruption since 1924. You have also United Water Resources, a New Jersey utility that has not missed a dividend for more than 100 years, since 1886.

All these companies get an A or A− rating from Standard & Poor's. You may note also that the banking companies mentioned above survived the stock market crash of 1929, the bank holiday of 1933, and the Great Depression of the 1930s. One of them, Norstar Bancorp., survived the War of 1812, the Civil War, both world wars, and various financial crashes and panics in between. These are not exactly fly-by-night companies.

Nor, to take one last example, is Hartford National Corporation. This is a bank holding company quoted over the counter and rated A− by Standard & Poor's. More than 100 mutual funds, pension funds, and other institutional investors own stock in this company. It has paid a dividend every year since 1927.

The Hartford National dividend reinvestment plan, says Kenneth N. Caesar, the company's investor relations officer, "allows an individual the opportunity to invest dividends and purchase stock at 95% of market value, as well as sending in cash investments up to $5,000 per quarter, also at a 5% discount.

"The plan allows the individual investors to sell a portion of their dividend reinvestment holdings and stay in the plan," he adds. So you are not locked into an inflexible prison cage of an investment for years and years. All you need to join the plan is to buy one share (in your own name, not the broker's), and from there on you can add as little as $25 a quarter—or nothing at all in fact—whenever you want to.

Larcenous Investors

By this time you may have an unholy gleam in your eye. If you can buy Hartford National shares at 95% of market value and then sell them in the stock market at 100%, you will have a nice 5% instant profit. Restrain such larcenous impulses.

Kenneth Caesar warns that Hartford "reserves the right to terminate participation if it is determined that arbitrage activities are being engaged in by an individual. Plan participation is closely monitored and shareholders who open duplicate accounts in either the same name, variations of the same name, or with the same tax identification number are advised that such activity is not allowed."

Other companies offering their shares at a discount have run into the same problem with sharp traders who know a built-in deal when they see one. Some companies have tightened up their rules like Hartford National, while others have dropped their discount offers.

Notwithstanding, there are still plenty of bargains around as this book is written. Here are some companies (including the six mentioned above) that currently offer you discounts on your reinvested dividends and also on your additional share purchases for cash:

American Security Corp. 5%
Bank of Virginia 5%
Banks of Mid-America Inc. 5%
California Real Estate Invest. Trust 5%
Carolina Power & Light 5%
Connecticut Water Service 5%
Energy North Inc. 5%

Equimark Corp. 5%
First American Corp. 5%
First of America Bank Corp. 5%
First Union Corp. 5%
First Wyoming Bancorp. 5%
Florida National Banks 5%
Hartford National Corp. 5%
Health Care REIT Inc. 4%
Hexcel Corp. 5%
Horizon Bancorp. 5%
Indian Head Banks Inc. 5%
Koger Co. 5%
Koger Partnership Ltd. 5%
Koger Properties Inc. 5%
Manhattan National Corp. 5%
Maryland National Corp. 5%
Meridian Bancorp. 5%
Multibank Financial Corp. 5% div., 3% cash
Norstar Bancorp Inc. 5%
Property Trust of America 5%
Santa Anita Realty Enterprises 5%
Storage Equities Inc. 5%
Sunwest Financial Services Inc. 5%
Texas Commerce Bankshares 5%
Tracor Inc. 5%
United Water Resources Inc. 5%
U.S. F & G Corp. 5%.

The above does not pretend to be an exhaustive list. There may be other similar bargains out there if you look around for them. There will almost certainly be additions to the list or deletions from it between the writing of this book and the date you read it.

If you need an updated list, one good source is Evergreen Enterprises, P.O. Box 763, Laurel MD 20707–0763; telephone 301-953-1861. Evergreen publishes an annual *Directory of Companies with Dividend Reinvestment Plans,* which costs $19.95. It also publishes a loose-leaf *Guide to Dividend Reinvestment Plans*. This is updated quarterly and costs $99 a year.

This whole scene is constantly changing as new companies introduce DRI plans while others modify or even phase out theirs. Sumie Kinoshita, who runs Evergreen, stresses that "investors should check first with the company before making any buying decisions. A person must be responsible for his or her own money and any decision to part with it."

Standard & Poor's, Public Relations Department, 25 Broadway, New York, NY 10004, has a periodically updated list of companies with dividend reinvestment plans for $2. For $1 so does United Business and Investment Service of 210 Newbury Street, Boston, MA 02116. However neither of these can match Evergreen's list in wealth of detail or frequency of updating. Standard & Poor's list is derived from its *The Outlook* weekly newsletter ($207 yearly subscription), which publishes the list twice a year.

Dividends at a Discount

The next-best bargain with regard to investment costs is the company that will give you a discount on the shares purchased with your reinvested dividends only. You have to pay full market price for the shares you buy with additional cash payments.

At the time of this writing there are at least 140 of these companies. They include:

Acme Electric Corp. 10%
Aetna Life & Casualty 5%
Amax Inc. 5%
Amsouth Bancorp 5%
Ball Corp. 5%
Bancoklahoma Corp. 5%
Bancorp Hawaii Inc. 5%
Bank of Boston 5%

Bank of Montreal 5%
Bank of New England Corp. 3%
Bank of New York Co. Inc. 5%
Bankers Trust New York Corp. 3%
Bell Canada Enterprises Inc. 5%
Bellsouth Corp. 5%
Beverly Enterprises 5%
Black Hills Power & Light 5%
BMJ Financial Corp. 5%
Bowater Inc. 5%
Bruncor Inc. 5%
California First Bank Inc. 5%
Canadian Imperial Bank of Commerce 5%
Carter Hawley Hale Stores Inc. 5%
Central Fidelity Banks 5%
Central Maine Power 5%
Central Vermont Public Service 5%
Century Telephone Enterprises 5%
Chase Manhattan Corp. 5%
Chemical New York Corp. 5%
Cityfed Financial Corp. 5%
Colonial Gas Co. 5%
Colorado National Bankshares Inc. 5%
Commonwealth Edison Co. 5%
Constellation Bancorp. 5%
CP National Corp. 5%
Dofasco Inc. 5%
Dominion Bankshares 5%
Dominion Textile Inc. 5%
Dravo Corp. 5%
Duquesne Light Co. 3%
Eastern Gas & Fuel Associates 5%
Eastern Utilities Associates 5%
Empire District Electric Co. 5%
Federal Realty Investment Trust 5%
First Bank System 5%
First Chicago Corp. 5%
First Fidelity Bancorp. 5%

First Jersey National Corp. 5%
First Maryland Bancorp. 5%
First Security Corp. 5%
First Virginia Banks Inc. 5%
Fleming Cos. Inc. 5%
Florida Progress Corp. 5%
Goodyear Tire & Rubber Co. 5%
Green Mountain Power Corp. 5%
Hawaiian Electric Industries 5%
Hibernia Corp. 5%
Holmes Co. Ltd. 5%
Hospital Corp. of America 5%
Huntington Bancshare Inc. 5%
Hydraulic Co. Inc. 5%
Illinois Power Co. Inc. 5%
Imperial Oil Ltd. 5%
Inco Ltd. 5%
Insilco Corp. 5%
Interfirst Corp. 5%
Interlake Inc. 5%
Irving Bank Corp. 5%
Jefferson Bankshares Inc. 5%
Kemper Corp. 5%
Kennametal Inc. 5%
Lafarge Corp. 5%
Landmark Bancshares Corp. 5%
Louisiana Power & Light Co. 5%
MacLean Hunter Ltd. 5%
Manufacturers National Corp. 5%
Marine Corp. 5%
Mayflower Corp. 5%
MCorp 5%
MDU Resources Group Inc. 5%
Mellon Bank Corp. 5%
Mercantile Bankshares Corp. 5%
Michigan Resources Co. 5%
Middle South Utilities Inc. 5%
Montana Power Co. 5%

MONY Real Estate Investors 5%
Moore Corp. Ltd. 5%
Morgan (J.P.) & Co. 5%
Mortgage & Realty Trust 5%
NCNB Corp. 5%
Nevada Power Co. 5%
New England Electric System 5%
New Plant Realty Trust 5%
North Carolina Natural Gas Corp. 5%
North Fork Bancorp. 5%
Northern Telecom Ltd. 5%
Norton Co. 5%
Norwest Corp. 5%
NUI Corp. 5%
Oneida Ltd. 5%
Oneok Inc. 5%
Panhandle Eastern 5%
Piedmont Natural Gas Co. 5%
PNC Financial Corp. 5%
Pro-Med Capital Inc. 5%
Public Service Co. of New Mexico 3%
Public Service Co. North Carolina 5%
Puget Sound Bancorp. 5%
Rainier Bancorp. 5%
Royal Bank of Canada 5%
Security Pacific Corp. 5%
Seibels Bruce Group 5%
Southeast Banking Corp. 5%
Southwestern Electric Service 5%
Sovran Financial Corp. 5%
Sun Electric Corp. 5%
Tenneco Inc. 5%
Texas American Bancshares 5%
Texas Utilities Co. 5%
Timken Co. 5%
Toronto Dominion Bank 5%
TransCanada Pipelines 5%
Travelers Corp. 5%

UGI Corp. 5%
United Cities Gas Co. 5%
United Virginia Bankshares Inc. 5%
Universal Foods Corp. 5%
Utilicorp United Inc. 5%
Valley Resources Inc. 5%
Warner Communications Inc. 5%
Washington Energy Co. 5%
Washington National Corp. 5%
Westcoast Transmission Co. Ltd. 5%

Companies That Don't Offer Discounts

And lastly there are the companies which provide dividend reinvestment plans but don't offer you any discounts on your purchases.

You will find them among several hundred stocks with DRI plans listed on the New York Stock Exchange, about sixty on the American Stock Exchange, and more than 100 on the over-the-counter market.

Companies With DRI Plans Listed on the NYSE

Abbott Laboratories
Acme-Cleveland Corp.
Adams Express Co.
Adams-Millis Corp.
Alcan Aluminium Ltd.
Alco Standard Corp.
Allegheny International Inc.
Allegheny Power System, Inc.
Allen Group Inc.
Allied Products Corp.
Allied-Signal Inc.

Allis-Chalmers Corp.
Alltel Corp.
Aluminum Co. of America
Amax Inc.
American Can Co.
American Capital Bond Fund
American Capital Convertible Securities
American Cyanamid Co.
American Electric Power Co.
American Express Co.
American General Corp.
American Heritage Life Investment Corp.
American Hoist & Derrick Co.
American Home Products Corp.
American Telephone & Telegraph Co.
Amfac Inc.
AMP Inc.
Anchor Hocking Corp.
Apache Corp.
Arkla Inc.
Armco Inc.
Armstrong World Industries
Arvin Industries
ASARCO Inc.
Ashland Oil, Inc.
Atlantic City Electric Co.
Atlantic Richfield Co.
Avnet Inc.
Avon Products, Inc.
AZP Group, Inc.
Baker International
Baltimore Gas & Electric Co.
BankAmerica Corp.
Barnes Group Inc.
Barnett Banks of Florida
Baxter Travenol Laboratories
Bay Financial Corp.
Bay State Gas Company

Becton Dickinson & Co.
Bell & Howell Co.
Bemis Company Inc.
Beneficial Corp.
Bethlehem Steel Corp.
Beverly Enterprises
Black & Decker Mfg. Co.
Boise Cascade Corp.
Borden, Inc.
Borg-Warner Corp.
Boston Edison Co.
Bristol-Myers Co.
Brockway Inc.
Brooklyn Union Gas Co.
Brown & Sharpe Manufacturing Co.
Brown Group, Inc.
Browning Ferris Industries, Inc.
Brunswick Corp.
Bunker Hill Income Securities
Burlington Industries, Inc.
Burlington Northern, Inc.
Burndy Corp.
Cabot Corp.
Canadian Pacific Ltd.
Carolina Freight Corp.
Carpenter Technology Corp.
Cascade Natural Gas Corp.
Castle & Cooke, Inc.
CBS Inc.
Centel Corp.
Centerior Energy Corp.
Central Hudson Gas & Electric Corp.
Central Illinois Public Service Co.
Central Louisiana Electric Co.
Central & South West Corp.
Champion International Corp.
Champion Spark Plug Co.
Chesapeake Corp.

Chevron Corp.
Chrysler Corp.
CIGNA Corp.
Cilcorp Inc.
Cincinnati Bell Inc.
Cincinnati Gas & Electric Co.
Cincinnati Milacron Inc.
Citicorp
Clark Equipment Co.
Cleveland Cliffs Inc.
Clorox Company
CNA Income Shares, Inc.
Coca-Cola Company
Colgate-Palmolive Co.
Colt Industries Inc.
Columbia Gas System Inc.
Combustion Engineering Inc.
Commonwealth Energy System
Conagra Inc.
Connecticut Energy Corp.
Connecticut Natural Gas Corp.
Conrac Corp.
Consolidated Edison of New York
Consolidated Natural Gas
Consumers Power Co.
Continental Corp.
Continental Illinois Corp.
Control Data Corp.
Cooper Industries Inc.
Copperweld Corp.
Corning Glass Works.
Corroon & Black Corp.
CP National Corp.
CPC International Inc.
Crompton & Knowles Corp.
CSX Corp.
Current Income Shares
Cyclops Corp.

Dana Corp.
Danaher Corp.
Day International
Dayton-Hudson Corp.
Deere & Co.
Delmarva Power & Light Co.
Delta Air Lines Inc.
Dennison Manufacturing Co.
Detroit Edison Co.
Dexter Corp.
Diamond Shamrock Corp.
DiGiorgio Corp.
Diversified Energies Inc.
Dominion Resources Inc.
Donnelly (R.R.) & Sons
Dow Chemical Co.
DPL Inc.
Dresser Industries Inc.
Drexel Bond-Debenture Trading Fund
Dreyfus Corp.
Duke Power Co.
du Pont de Nemours (E.I.) & Co.
Eagle-Picher Industries
Eastman Kodak Co.
Eaton Corp.
EG & G Co.
Emerson Electric Co.
Emery Air Freight Corp.
Emhart Corp.
Enserch Corp.
Entex Inc.
Equifax, Inc.
Equitable Resources, Inc.
Ethyl Corp.
Excelsior Income Shares Inc.
Exxon Corp.
Fairchild Industries, Inc.
Federal Company

Federal-Mogul Corp.
Federal National Mortgage Association
Federal Paper Board Co., Inc.
Federated Department Stores Inc.
Ferro Corp.
Firestone Tire & Rubber Co.
First City Bancorporation of Texas
First Interstate Bancorp.
First Mississippi Corp.
First Pennsylvania Corp.
First Union Real Estate Eq. & Mtge.
First Wisconsin Corp.
Fleet Financial Group Inc.
FMC Corp.
Foote, Cone & Belding Communications
Ford Motor Co.
Fort Dearborn Income Securities.
Fort Howard Paper Co.
Foster Wheeler Corp.
Foxboro Company
FPL Group Inc.
GAF Corp.
Gannett Co. Inc.
GATX Corp.
Gencorp Inc.
General American Investors Co.
General Cinema Corp.
General Electric Co.
General Mills Inc.
General Motors Corp.
General Public Utilities Corp.
General Signal Corp.
Georgia-Pacific Corp.
Gerber Products Co.
Gillette Co.
Gleason Works
Goodrich (B.F.) & Co.
Gordon Jewelry Corp.

Gould Inc.
Grace (W.R.) & Co.
Great Northern Nekoosa Corp.
Great Western Financial Corp.
Grow Group Inc.
Grumman Corp.
GTE Corp.
Gulf States Utilities Co.
Gulf & Western Industries
Handy & Harman
Harnischefeger Corp.
Harris Corp.
Harsco Corp.
Hartmarx Corp.
Hatteras Income Securities
Hayes-Albion Corp.
Hercules Inc.
Hershey Foods Corp.
Holly Sugar Corp.
Homestake Mining Co.
Honeywell Inc.
Houghton Mifflin Co.
Household International Inc.
Houston Ind. Inc.
HRE Properties
Hughes Tool Co.
Humana Inc.
IC Industries Inc.
Idaho Power Co.
Ideal Basic Industries
Illinois Power Co.
INA Investment Securities Inc.
Ingersoll Rand Co.
Inter Capital Income Securities
International Business Machines
International Minerals & Chemicals
International Multifoods Corp.
International Paper Co.

Interpublic Group of Companies, Inc.
Interstate Power Co.
Iowa-Illinois Gas & Electric Co.
Iowa Resources
IPALCO Industries, Inc.
IRT Property Co.
ITT Corp.
IU International Corp.
Japan Fund Inc.
Jefferson Pilot Corp.
John Hancock Income Securities
John Hancock Investor Inc.
Johnson Controls, Inc.
Jorgensen (Earl M.) Co.
Jostens Inc.
Joy Manufacturing Co.
Kaiser Aluminum & Chemical Corp.
Kaneb Services
Kansas City Gas & Electric.
Kansas City Power & Light
Kaufman & Broad Inc.
Kentucky Utilities Co.
Kerr-McGee Corp.
Key Corp.
Kidde Inc.
Kimberly Clark Corp.
KN Energy Inc.
Kollmorgen Corp.
Koppers Co.
Kroger Co.
Kuhlman Corp.
Leaseway Transportation
Lehman Corp.
Lincoln National Corp.
Lincoln National Direct Placement Fund
LLC Corp.
Long Island Lighting Co.
Louisiana-Pacific Corp.

Lucky Stores Inc.
Lukens Steel Co.
Macmillan Inc.
Manhattan Industries Inc.
Manufacturers Hanover Corp.
Manville Corp.
Mapco Inc.
Marine Midland Banks Inc.
Marion Laboratories
Marsh & McLennan Co.
Massmutual Income Investors
Maxxam Group Inc.
Maytag Co.
McKesson Inc.
Mead Corp.
Merck & Co.
Merrill Lynch & Co.
Minnesota Mining & Manufacturing
Minnesota Power & Light
Mobil Corp.
Mohasco Corp.
Monsanto Co.
Montgomery Street Income Securities
Moore McCormack Resources
Morrison Knudsen Corp.
Motorola Inc.
Munford Inc.
Munsingwear Inc.
Murray Ohio Mfg.
Mutual of Omaha Interest Shares
National Distillers & Chemical Corp.
National Fuel & Gas
National Intergroup
National Medical Enterprises
National Standard Co.
Navistar International Corp.
NBD Bancorp.
NCR Corp.

New Jersey Resources Corp.
New York State Electric & Gas
Newhall Land & Farming Co.
Newmont Mining Corp.
Niagara Mohawk Power Co.
Niagara Shares Corp.
Nicor Inc.
NL Industries
Norstar Bancorp.
Northeast Utilities
Northern Indiana Public Service
Northern States Power Co.
Nucor Corp.
Nynex Corp.
Oakite Products Inc.
Occidental Petroleum Corp.
Ogden Corp.
Ohio Edison Co.
Oklahoma Gas & Electric Co.
Olin Corp.
Orange Co. Inc.
Orange & Rockland Utilities
Outboard Marine Corp.
Owens-Corning Fiberglass
Owens Illinois Inc.
Pacific American Income Shares
Pacific Gas & Electric Co.
Pacific Lighting Corp.
Pacific Telesis Group
Pacificorp
Paine Webber Group
Penney (J.C.) & Co.
Pennsylvania Power & Light
Pennwalt Corp.
Pennzoil Co.
Peoples Energy Corp.
Pepsico Inc.
Petroleum & Resources Corp.

Pfizer Inc.
Phelps Dodge Corp.
Philadelphia Electric Co.
Philadelphia Suburban Corp.
Phillip Morris Cos.
Pier I Inc.
Pillsbury Co.
Pitney Bowes Inc.
Portland General Corp.
Potlatch Corp.
Potomac Electric Power Co.
PPG Industries Inc.
Public Service Co. of Colorado
Public Service Co. of Indiana
Public Service Co. of New Hampshire
Public Service Electric & Gas Co.
Pueblo International
Puget Sound Power & Light Co.
Quaker Oats Co.
Quaker State Oil Refining Co.
Quanex Corp.
Questar Corp.
Ranco Inc.
Ralston Purina Co.
Raytheon Co.
Reading & Bates Corp.
Republicbank Corp.
Rexham Corp.
Rexnord Inc.
Reynolds Metals Co.
RJR Nabisco
RLC Corp.
Rochester Gas & Electric Corp.
Rochester Telephone Corp.
Rockwell International Corp.
Rohr Industries Inc.
Rollins Inc.
Rorer Group

Ryder Systems Inc.
St. Joseph Light & Power Co.
San Diego Gas & Electric Co.
Santa Anita Realty Enterprises
Sara Lee Corp.
Saul Real Estate Investment Trust
Savannah Electric & Power Co.
Scana Corp.
Schering-Plough Corp.
Scott Paper Co.
Sealed Power Corp.
Sears, Roebuck & Co.
Shaklee Corp.
Sherwin-Williams Co.
Sierra Pacific Resources
Smith International Inc.
Smithkline Corp.
Smucker (J.M.) Co.
Sonat Inc.
South Jersey Ind.
Southern California Edison Co.
Southern Co.
Southern Indiana Gas & Electric Co.
Southern New England Telephone Co.
Southwest Gas Corp.
Southwestern Public Service
Squibb Corp.
Standard Oil Co.
Standex International
Stanley Works
State Mutual Securities
Sterling Drug Inc.
Stevens (J.P.) & Co.
Stewart-Warner Corp.
Stone & Webster Inc.
Stop & Shop Cos.
Storage Equities Inc.
Stride Rite Corp.

Sun Company
Sundstrand Corp.
Taft Broadcasting Co.
Talley Industries
Teco Energy
Texaco Inc.
Texas Eastern Corp.
Textron Inc.
Thackeray Corp.
Thomas & Betts Corp.
Tidewater Inc.
Tiger International
Time Inc.
TNP Enterprises
Toro Co.
Transamerica Corp.
Transamerica Income Shares
TransCanada Pipelines
Transcon Inc.
Trico Industries
Tri-Continental Corp.
TRW Inc.
Tucson Electric Power Co.
Twin Disc Inc.
Union Camp Corp.
Union Carbide Corp.
Union Corp.
Union Electric Co.
Union Pacific Corp.
United Illuminating Co.
United Jersey Banks
Unocal Corp.
USF & G
USG Corp.
U.S. Leasing
United States Shoe Corp.
United States Tobacco Co.
United Telecommunications

Universal Leaf Tobacco
Upjohn Co.
USLife Corp.
US Life Income Fund
Utah Power & Light Co.
Van Dorn Co.
Varian Associates
Vestaur Securities
VF Corp.
Vulcan Materials Inc.
Walgreen Co.
Walt Disney Co.
Walter (Jim) Corp.
Warner Lambert
Washington Gas & Light
Washington Water Power Co.
Weis Markets Inc.
Wells Fargo & Co.
Wells Fargo Mortgage & Realty Trust
Wendy's International
Western Union Corp.
Westvaco Corp.
Weyerhaeuser Co.
Whirlpool Corp.
Wicor Inc.
Williams Cos.
Winn-Dixie Stores
Wisconsin Electric Power
Wisconsin Power & Light
Wisconsin Public Service Co.
Witco Chemical Corp.
Woolworth & Co.
Wrigley (Wm.) Jr. Co.
Wyle Laboratories
Xerox Corp.
Zenith Electronics

Here again, there may be changes in the list between the time this book is written and the time you

read it. The New York Stock Exchange has not been updating its list in 1987, but you could ask the Exchange if it has an updated list by the time you read this (New York Stock Exchange, Communications Services, 11 Wall Street, New York, NY 10005).

American Stock Exchange
Companies with DRI Plans

On the AMEX, the following companies offer dividend reinvestment plans as this is written, according to the Exchange:

Aluminum Co. of America
American Express Co.
American Petrofina Inc.
Bancroft Convertible Fund
Bank Building & Equipment
Brown-Forman Inc.
California REIT
Castle Convertible Fund Inc.
Champion Products Inc.
Chicago Rivet & Machine Co.
Citizens First Bancorp.
Copley Properties Inc.
Countrywide Mortgage Investments Inc.
Curtice-Burns, Inc.
Del-Val Financial Corp.
Dillard Department Stores
Domtar Inc.
The Eastern Company
Equity Income Fund
First Wyoming Bancorporation
Firstcorp Inc.
Fitchburg Gas & Electric Light Co.
Giant Food, Inc.
Gorman-Rupp Company
Hannaford Brothers Co.
Health Care REIT, Inc.

Hotel Properties, Inc.
HUBCO, Inc.
Inter-City Gas Corporation
International Income Property Inc.
Koger Company
Landmark Bancshares Corp.
Lear Petroleum Partners L.P.
Media General Inc.
Money Management Corporation
Mortgage Investments Plus, Inc.
New Plan Realty Trust
New York Times Co.
Newport Electric
NRM Energy Company
Pall Corporation
Peerless Tube Co.
Penn Traffic Company
Penril Corp.
Presidential Realty Corp.
Providence Energy Corp.
Ransburg Corp.
Realty South Investors Inc.
Russell Corp.
SJW Corp.
Seton Company
Standard Products Co.
Telephone & Data Systems Inc.
Turner Equity Investors Inc.
UNITIL Corp.
Valley Resources Inc.
VMS Short Term Income Trust
Washington REIT
Del E. Webb Investment Properties Inc.
Wedgestone Realty Investors Trust

For an updated version of the Amex list you might
contact the American Stock Exchange, Rulings and Inquiries Department, 86 Trinity Place, New York, NY
10006.

A sampling of OTC stocks offering dividend reinvestment plans turns up more than 100 companies, a surprisingly large proportion of which are rated A− A, or even A+ by Standard & Poor's:

Acceleration Corp.
Accuray Corp.
Addison Wesley Publishing Co.
Allied Bancshares Inc.
American Aggregates Corp.
American Federal Savings Loan of Colorado
American Filtrona
American Fletcher Co.
American Greetings Corp.
Ameritrust Corp.
Atlanta Gas Light Co.
Bank South Corp.
Banta (George) Co.
BayBanks Inc.
Berkshire Gas Co.
Boatmen's Bancshares
Bob Evans Farms
Branch Corp.
Business Men's Assurance Co. of America
Butler Manufacturing Co.
CB & T Bancshares Inc.
CCB Financial
Centerre Bancorp.
Central Bancorp of Cincinnati
Central Bancshares of the South
Cincinnati Financial Corp.
Citizens & Southern Corp.
Citizens Fidelity Corp.
Citytrust Nacorp.
Coca-Cola Bottling Co. Consolidated
Comerica Inc.

Commercial Bancshares Inc.
Conifer Group
Consolidated Capital Special Trust
Consumers Water Co.
Continental Bancorp.
CoreStates Financial Corp.
Cross & Trecker Corp.
Dunkin' Donuts
Duriron Co.
Economics Laboratory Inc.
El Paso Electric Co.
Fifth Third Bancorp.
Figgie International
First Alabama Bancshares
First Bancorp of Ohio
First Commerce Corp.
First Continental REIT
First Empire State
First Executive
First Interstate Corp. of Wisconsin
First Interstate of Iowa
First Kentucky National Corp.
First National Cincinnati
First NH Banks
First Tennessee National
Fourth Financial Corp.
Fuller (H.B.) Co.
Godfrey Co.
Goulds Pumps Inc.
Hartford Steam Boiler Insurance
Hawkeye Bancorp.
Justin Industries
Kaman Corp.
Lance Inc.
Lincoln Telecommunications
Louisiana Bancshares
Madison Gas & Electric Co.
Mark Twain Bancshares

Marsh Supermarkets
Marshall & Ilsley Corp.
McCormick & Co.
Mercantile Bancorp Inc.
Middlesex Water Co.
Midlantic Banks Inc.
Millipore Corp.
Mobile Gas Service Corp.
Nash Finch Co.
National City Corp.
National Data Corp.
Northwest Natural Gas
Ogilvy Group
Ohio Casualty Corp.
Old National Bancorp.
Old Republic International Corp.
Old Stone Corp.
Otter Tail Power Co.
Pennsylvania Enterprises
Pentair Inc.
Pioneer Hi-Bred International
Revere AE Capital Fund
Roadway Services Inc.
Rose's Stores
RPM Inc.
St. Paul Cos.
Savannah Foods & Industries
Security Bancorp.
Shawmut Corp.
Simpson Industries
Society Corp.
Sonoco Products
Southern California Water Co.
SouthTrust Corp.
State Street Boston Corp.
Stewart Information Services
Summit Bancorporation
U.S. Bancorp.

Upper Peninsula Power Co.
USLICO Corp.
USP Real Estate Investment Trust
Valley Bancorporation
Valley National Corp.
Victoria Bankshares
WestAmerica Bancorp.
Wetterau Inc.
Wisconsin Southern Gas
Wolverine Technologies
Zions Utah Bancorp.

One Last Word

When you know that you can invest in companies one share at a time any day you have $10 to $50 to spare, there may be a big temptation to go on an investing spree. There is at least one enthusiast, Duane Frederic, who has a portfolio of more than 300 companies, mostly bought one share at a time initially so as to get into the companies' dividend reinvestment plans. Contain your enthusiasm. Spreading investments around on that scale is going to snow you under with paper work. It is also going to give you a major headache when the time comes to make out your income tax return. Your tax return might need four or five extra pages for dividend statements. And your tax preparer's fee from H & R Block will probably soak up the dividends from 150 to 200 of your one-share investments.

All your dividends, incidentally, will be taxed as ordinary income for the year in which they are paid. So will any discounts on the shares you bought through reinvestment or cash purchase.

You may be able to make an end run around your broker, but don't try it with the IRS. You can always dump your broker, but you can't get rid of your tax inspector so easily.

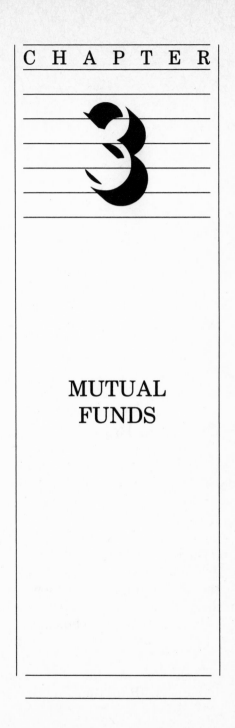

CHAPTER

3

MUTUAL
FUNDS

On the Average, Less
Than You Bargained For

There are now about 2,000 mutual funds in the United States. Believe it or not, they outnumber the 1,500 or so stocks on the New York Stock Exchange—and they are still proliferating like rabbits. In 1986, 370 new funds came to market—more than one a day. Mutual funds' assets took fifty-five years to reach the $100 billion mark in 1979. By 1987 American investors had poured so much money into them that fund assets topped $700 billion and were headed for an eightfold increase in eight years. About 25 million American households now own mutual fund shares, held in about 40 million individual accounts.

Obviously, American investors have had a passionate love affair going with mutual funds in the last few years, and they certainly have a huge and growing array of funds to choose from. But are they getting a good deal from the mutual fund industry?

On the average, no. The average mutual fund spends a lot of money running the fund and paying professional stock-pickers to beat the market. And then it ends up underperforming the market. Lipper Analytical Services, Inc., a firm that specializes in statistical data on mutual funds, recorded these melancholy figures:

As of December 31, 1986, the 1,117 mutual funds Lipper keeps track of registered a median gain of 13.99% from January 1, 1986. (The median means that half the funds did better and half did worse than that 13.99% gain.) There is not one major general market index that did not do better than this in 1986. The Wilshire 5,000 Stock Index, which covers 5,000 American companies, gained 16.10%. Standard & Poor's Index of 500 Stocks was up 18.57%. The S&P 500 Index covers about 70% of the value of all stocks traded in the United States, and presumably anybody with any sort of investment skill should be able to beat this unmanaged group of stocks even if they are unable to match the Wilshire 5,000, which covers practically the entire market. The Dow Jones average of thirty industrial stocks, which includes thirty of the biggest American corporations, rose a whopping 27.25% in 1986. (In all the cases given above, by the way, the figures include stock prices plus reinvested dividends.) The median mutual fund was also unable to match the S&P 500 Index over the previous three months, over the previous five years, over the previous ten years, and over the previous fifteen years, all the way back to December 31, 1971.

Lipper has a breakdown of the 1,117 mutual funds into eighteen categories—growth funds, small company funds, income funds, utility funds, specialty funds, and so on. Over the fifteen-year 1971–1986 period, in only seven of the eighteen categories was the average fund able to beat the S&P 500 stock average.

The average investor could pick stocks at random from the 500 companies in the S&P index, save the mutual fund costs, and might end up doing as well or better by himself than the average mutual fund does for him. If he bought stocks through company dividend reinvestment plans and thus paid no brokerage commissions, he might well do better than the average mutual fund, for the simple reason that dividend reinvestment plans have practically no transaction costs. A mutual fund does have transaction costs, as well as administrative costs—sometimes very large costs, as we shall see further on. It is true that a mutual fund with 50 to 100 stocks in its portfolio would have greater diversification than the average investor could achieve on his own without running into a lot of paper work keeping track of 50 to 100 individual stocks. But one does not really need that much diversification. A study in the *Journal of Finance* by J. L. Evans and S. H. Archer established years ago that the amount of risk reduction obtainable through the addition of stocks to a portfolio diminishes very quickly beyond a certain point. They found very little risk reduction is achieved after the portfolio contains about fifteen to twenty common stocks spread over a variety of different industries.

However, you are not the average investor; nor is your mutual fund necessarily the average mutual fund. The question is how are **you** doing with your particular fund, and how can you do better? If you are a holder of Fidelity Magellan Fund (up 1,721% in value in the fifteen years from 1971 to 1986) you have gotten an outstanding deal. If you bought Steadman American Industry Fund in 1971 (down 37% over the same fifteen years) you would have done better to stick your money under the mattress.

The fact is, it all depends on which particular fund you bought then and which one you buy now.

You may note, in passing, that the favorite argument for mutual funds, greater stability through diversification, does not seem to work all that well. Imagine that you had bought two individual stocks in 1971, any stocks at all. Do you really think that you could have come out with any wider discrepancy of results than Magellan's plus 1,721% and Steadman's minus 37%?

So how do you choose your mutual fund?

The first conclusion that naturally springs to mind is that if a mutual fund has had an outstanding track record in the past, then it will continue to outrun the pack in the future. But this does not always work out too well, as any greyhound racetrack bettor can tell you, particularly over fairly short periods. Yesterday's winner is not infrequently tomorrow's dog. United Services Gold Shares, for instance, was at the top of the heap among no-load mutual funds in 1979, and was number one again in 1982, an unprecedented double crown. But in 1985 it fell near the bottom in performance, only to bounce back near the top in 1986. Since United Services Gold Shares specializes in the shares of gold-mining companies, this fund did well when the price of gold went up and badly when the price of gold went down. Basically, it's as simple as that. If you had a crystal ball to tell you what the price of gold will be in the coming year, you would have a pretty good idea of what this fund's performance will be over the next twelve months. Without such a clear vision of the future, there is no way of telling.

There is no sure way of telling, either, how any of the other 2,000 funds are going to do in the future. Most of them invest exclusively in American companies. If the U.S. economy does well, and the stock market rises with it, these mutual funds are going to make money for you. But even professional economists are invariably unable to agree on what is in store for the economy, and like investment advisers they gaze into crystal balls that are usually cracked, cloudy, and warped. As for the stock market, there are contrary-minded investors who go so far as to sell stocks when the majority of professional investment advisers say the market will go up because they know that the majority of professional investment advisers are nearly always wrong. There is, as we have seen, actual statistical proof of this over a period as long as fifteen years. In fact if you want to confirm that this happens in the short term too, you could buy *Barron's* magazine and turn to the back pages. You will find there a table headed Lipper Mutual Fund Performance Averages. In a January 1987 issue of *Barron's,* for example, which recorded a week of outstanding price advances in the stock market, the Dow Jones 30 Industrials Average was up 8.23% (including reinvested dividends) and the S&P 500 Stock Index was up 5.67% (also with reinvested dividends). In that same week, the best the average growth fund could do was +3.03%, the average growth and income fund +2.88%, the average balanced fund +2.02%, the average science and technology fund +5.62%, and the average international fund +2.43%. On the average, laggards in every category of fund except the gold funds, whose average 6.17% gain for the week managed to beat the S&P 500 but not the Dow Jones.

So the average fund pays a lot of high-priced financial talent to pick stocks that don't even keep up with the general market. A chimpanzee throwing darts at the newspaper stock tables could make a better selection on average. As there are already mutual funds specializing in everything from casualty insurance stocks to computer software stocks, any day now we are going to see our First Chimpanzee Fund. (Indeed, in a sense we already have such a fund under a more respectable name, as we shall see further on).

Meanwhile, if practically nobody else can consistently predict the future with any confidence—or at least with any great profitability in the mutual fund industry—why should we think that we can?

So, what if we abandon the clairvoyant, peer-into-the-future approach? There may perhaps be some other way of picking mutual funds that are probable winners. And in fact there is. It doesn't involve crystal balls; it involves pennypinching.

As Benjamin Franklin implied, a person who watches his pennies over a long period of time is going to end up rich and anyone who squanders his money is going to end up in the poorhouse.

The same bleak truth applies to mutual funds and to mutual fund investors. Avoid any fund that charges you too much for its services and that tends to throw your money around with abandon. The results of such a simpleminded, puritanical approach toward mutual fund profligacy may surprise you very much—as you will see at the end of this chapter.

So let's go on with our Scrooge act and put the mutual fund industry through the financial wringer.

Load Funds: They Cost You 8.5%—Oops, 9.3%

First through the wringer are the load funds, which we place first because they have salespeople, who take the initiative and are persistent. A load fund is going to take 8.5% of your money right off the top and you are never going to see it again. This money—your money—is going into the salesperson's pocket. Actually, the truth is even worse than that. When a fund tells you its sales commission is 8.5%, this is not strictly true. The reason is that if you invest $10,000 in a fund and $850 is taken out as commission, then your net investment is only $9,150. And an $850 commission on your $9,150 investment works out to 9.3%, not 8.5%.

None of this $850 commission is going to do you any

good. It is not paying for investment research or broker-age expenses or anything else that is of any value to you. It is purely a reward to the salesperson who talked you into buying this particular fund and to the firm that distributes its shares. So why pay a 9.3% commission?

Usually there is no good reason to do so. One study after another over the past twenty-five years has demonstrated the obvious, that there is no difference in the average performance of load funds and no-load funds. The people who run no-loads are just as likely to be competent or incompetent as those who run load funds. The major difference, as the Wharton School of Finance pointed out a quarter of a century ago in a 1962 study, is that "fund shareholders paying higher sales charges had a less favorable investment experience than those paying less." Could anything be more obvious and predictable?

Over a long period of time, this investment disadvantage of the load mutual fund is compounded into thousands of dollars. Investor Gilbert, let us say, uses a no-load fund for his Individual Retirement Account, while investor Sullivan puts his money into a load fund. Both investors contribute the maximum amount allowed by law, $2,000 a year, and both funds do equally well—a 10% annual return on each. The difference is that Gilbert gets all his $2,000 invested every year, while Sullivan gets to put in only $1,830 after his 8.5% load fund commission is taken out. This difference is only $170 a year, but over a thirty-year working life it builds up to a difference of $33,811. Both Gilbert and Sullivan put a total of $60,000 into their IRAs over their working lives, but Gilbert ends up with an investment of $397,784 while Sullivan has only $363,973.

While Gilbert sings for joy and Sullivan dances in frustration, let us record that no farsighted, self-respecting penny-pinching investor would ever put money into a load fund if there were anything cheaper available. And there are other funds available.

Low-Load Funds:
They Cost You 2% to 5%

A somewhat better bargain is the low-load fund, which typically charges 2% to 3%, sometimes even 4% or 5%, when you buy. Some low-loads were originally no-loads that weren't quite making a go of it for the management company, so management decided to add a small sales charge to beef up its income. Other low-loads got that way because the fund was doing so well that the management company figured it could add the sales charge without scaring off potential investors, and got away with it in view of the fund's good track record.

Many funds claim that marketing costs force them to add the "low" loads. But as the American Association of Individual Investors said in its 1985 annual *Guide to No-Load Mutual Funds,* "These charges are added to create profits for the fund distributor. Often this is a parent corporation of the management company" that runs the fund.

In any event, let us not get into this argument. For a penny-pinching investor there are better bargains around than low-loads.

No-Load Funds:
Cost to You, in Theory, 0%—
In Practice, Watch Out!

The no-load fund charges you no purchase commission at all. The advantage of this is so obvious that no-loads have been gaining constantly on the load funds in recent years. Now they represent about half the funds on the market. The only wonder, really, is that any load funds still exist at this stage of the game.

If you look up the list of mutual fund quotations in your local newspaper or the *Wall Street Journal,* you may think perhaps that the letters NL, which distinguish the no-load funds, mark out the frontiers of the mutual fund investor's Promised Land. Alas, this is not so.

Back-End Load Funds: They Cost You 1% to 6%

It turns out that some of the NLs are not really no-loads at all. If you examine the table of mutual fund quotations carefully, all the way down to the bottom, you will discover that some of the NLs are more like scorpions— they have a sting in the tail. These are back-end load funds. They may lure you in with the NL designation, but then they hit you with a commission when you try to get out. That is, they charge you a redemption fee when you sell your shares. The mark of the beast is the little letter r next to the fund's name. If you glance at the explanations at the bottom of the table you find that r means that "a redemption charge may apply."

Even this warning is inadequate, however. The lists of daily mutual fund quotations are provided to newspapers by the two main news agencies that serve the American press, the Associated Press and United Press International. Either because AP and UPI do not provide the information or because the newspapers omit it for reasons of space, some of the hidden-load funds get themselves quoted as genuine no-loads. As many as 10% of the hidden-load funds may be getting themselves quoted as genuine no-loads.

A few funds have always had these fees, usually 1% to 2%, to discourage in-and-out trading in the fund's shares. If you bought into the fund and then sold for a quick profit within two or six months or in some cases one year of your purchase, you would pay the penalty. After that time you can sell without being nicked for your pint of blood. The justification offered is that the portfolio manager cannot do a good job if he is being hit all the time by the sales of antsy investors. Perhaps so, but is the fund run for the management's convenience or for yours?

And now some enterprising funds have improved on this system—improved, that is, from their point of view. They have upped the redemption fee to 5% or 6% and extended the penalty period out to five years or so. Should you sell your shares in the first year, for instance, you would pay a 6% redemption fee, then 5% in the second year, 4% in the third, and so on.

These back-end loads may still seem lower than the usual 8.5% front-end load, but they may turn out to be more. Invest $1,000 in the Superduper Fund, for instance. It turns in a superduper investment performance so that your holding is worth $3,000 in four years, and then you are going to pay 3% redemption fee, which by this time equals 9% of your initial investment.

"We believe this practice is deceptive and exploitative," says a study by the American Association of Individual Investors.

Hidden-Load Funds: They Cost You 0.25% to 1.25%—Every Year

Exploitative or not, the back-end load fund does, at least sometimes, have that little r warning flag on its back to alert you that it charges a redemption fee. The hidden-load fund gives you no such warning in the newspaper list of quotations. You have to read the fund's prospectus—and sometimes you have to scan that document very carefully—to find the warning symbol, which in this case is 12b-1.

Search carefully through the fund's prospectus for information on 12b-1. This is not something the fund particularly wants you to know about, and it may be hidden deep in the fine print. And when you do find it, the explanation may be so abbreviated that you would have to write to the fund and ask for its "Statement of Additional Information." This document comes free of charge, but it will not come at all unless you ask for it.

The 12b-1 plans are named after a Securities and Exchange Commission ruling on mutual funds in force since 1980. The rule allows fund management to raid the fund's assets (your assets) to cover its marketing, promotional, and advertising expenses. Rule 12b-1 does not specify the maximum amount that can be spent on this, and some funds are spending more than 1% of fund assets per year.

The SEC is the securities industry's watchdog agency, and in general it does a fairly good job of watching out for you when you venture out into the mutual fund jungle. It enforces laws passed in the 1930s and 1940s to ensure that the funds are managed and operated in the best interests of the shareholders. All mutual funds have to register with the SEC, and they are not allowed to sell their wares without first providing you with a prospectus containing full disclosure of the fund's management, investment aims, purchase and redemption procedures, portfolio investments, and other business practices. But 12b-1 is a rathole where the watchdogs nodded and let the varmints in to nibble away at your money.

This little gimmick has spread like the plague through the ranks of mutual funds, both load and no-load. More than 600 funds now have 12b-1 plans, which you should note are not one-shot costs like sales commissions. When you buy a 12b-1 fund your investment is going to be drained year in and year out by anything from 0.25% to 1.25%.

Over a period of time the 12b-1 can be just as expensive as the 8.5% load. The *Handbook for No-Load Fund Investors* gives this example: you have two no-load funds, one with a 12b-1 plan which takes 1% a year, and the other without a 12b-1 plan. The latter grows at a 10%

yearly rate, while the 12b-1 fund grows at only 9% because of the 1% yearly fee. You start out with a $10,000 investment. After ten years the fund without the 12b-1 plan has grown to $25,937, while the 12b-1 fund is worth only $23,674. The *Handbook* points out that if you had bought a fund with an 8.5% load but no 12b-1 plan, you would have come out about the same as with the 12b-1 no-load. So over the long term, the reasons for avoiding 12b-1 plan funds are just as strong as they are for avoiding load funds.

The way these 12b-1 exactions came about is that the mutual fund industry talked its way into a sweetheart of a deal. Every fund charges a management fee, which traditionally has been used to cover marketing and distribution costs, such as printing and mailing prospectuses, advertising, and paying sales personnel and dealers. It occurred to some enterprising management companies that they could make a lot more money if they shoved these expenses off onto the mutual fund investor. They argued, believe it or not, that this would be good for the fund investor because it would help the fund to grow bigger and thus better able to benefit from the economies of larger-scale operation. And, believe it or not, the SEC bought this argument.

Until something is done about 12b-1, the only thing you can do is to avoid such funds, even if, as some of them claim, they are not actually charging as much as they are entitled to under the 12b-1 provisions, or in fact not charging anything at all.

Expense Ratios: They Cost You from 0.5% to More Than 4% a Year

So far we have been talking basically about one thing only: what your fund is going to cost you in marketing expenses—front-end load, low-load, back-end load, hidden-load. This is by no means the end of the matter, however. It is not only expensive to market a fund, it also costs money—in some cases an awful lot of money—to run one. And you, dear shareholder, are going to bear the greater part of this expense.

Your fund is going to charge you for management advisory fees and administrative expenses. These are added together and deducted from the fund's assets (your assets).

The adviser's fee covers the cost of providing investment advice, office space, bookkeeping, statistical and clerical services, executive salaries, and promotional expenses. The fund adviser or management corporation traditionally received a fee of 0.5% of average fund assets. However, newer and more aggressive funds have improved on this too: they have set fees of 0.75% or even 1%. It has been estimated that at 0.5% a fund must accumulate $100 million in assets before the operation becomes profitable for the management company. Nevertheless, many fund management companies have stables of funds, some as many as thirty, to share the costs. The management fee is usually set on a declining scale as assets increase, for example, 0.5% up to $250 million in assets, then 0.45% on assets in excess of $250 million, and so on. This tends to make larger funds cheaper for the fund investor.

In addition, the fund (that is to say you and your fellow investors) pays a number of other costs directly, such as mailing and printing expenses for prospectuses and other material for shareholders, legal and auditing fees, custodian and transfer agent fees, and the expenses of independent directors.

All of the above is combined into the fund's "ratio of expenses to average net assets," a figure the fund is required to include in its prospectus.

According to the *Handbook for No-Load Fund Inves-*

tors, the average expense ratio of common stock funds in 1986 was 1.09%, with the larger funds showing proportionately lower ratios than smaller ones. Funds with more than $500 million in assets had an average ratio of 0.73%, funds with $10 million or less an average 1.71%. For bond funds the ratio tended to be lower, with an average of 0.87%. Even the smaller bond funds with $10 million assets or less had a ratio of 1.06%—less than the average of all common stock funds. The *Individual Investor's Guide to No-Load Mutual Funds* came up with somewhat similar figures: an average 1.12% for common stock no-load funds, 1.02% for bond funds. It found that the average management fee was 0.6%.

The expense ratio, incidentally, is limited to a maximum set by each state. The more restrictive states have a top rate of 1.5%. All fund contracts require the investment adviser to reimburse the shareholders for expenditures that go over the state maximum, so funds with high expense ratios tend not to register in states that treat them too severely in this matter.

The *Handbook for No-Load Fund Investors* comments that "while there's no doubt that superior management can overcome the drag of a high expense ratio in a given month, or even over a two- or three-year period, we don't believe there are many fund managers who can offset this drag over a long period of time."

The *Handbook* lists seventeen funds that had an expense ratio of 2% or higher in 1984 and shows their five-year performance history up to that time. Only three out of seventeen ranked above average. Most of the other fourteen were far below average, eight of them in the bottom 10% of the rankings.

The lesson is clear: when choosing your mutual fund, check its expense ratio over the past five years. In the fund's prospectus, be sure to look for the expense ratio in a section usually headed Per Share Income and Capital Changes.

If the ratio is higher than the average, say over 1.1%, don't buy the fund.

Transaction Costs: They Cost You ?% to ?% a Year

Add up all the percentages we have accumulated so far in commission costs, advisory fees, and administrative expenses. Think the total is too high already? Brace yourself for more. We still haven't gotten to a mutual fund's real business costs: the buying and selling of shares.

One of the big arguments usually made for mutual funds is that they can save on commission costs by buying and selling big blocks of shares. The individual investor, it is argued, would pay proportionately higher brokerage costs dealing in lots of 100 or 1,000 shares. This seems plausible at first sight, but doesn't always hold up under closer scrutiny.

A study by Wells Fargo Investment Advisors indicates that the total round-trip transaction cost (that is, purchase and sale) of a 10,000-share block at $50 a share averages about 4%. The study found that the bigger the block, the higher the transaction costs. The reason is that it is harder to find a ready market for 10,000 shares at one go than it is for 100 shares. So the mutual fund, or any other big financial institution, trying to buy or sell a large block has to offer the broker price concessions. The fund has to sell at a lower price or buy at a higher price in order to make a deal. And the price concession is only partially compensated by lower brokerage commissions on large lots.

This does not necessarily show up on the fund's prospectus, however. Mutual funds are usually remarkably reticent about giving you actual dollar costs of the brokerage commissions they have to pay. A fund might occasionally tell you that the average brokerage commission it paid was 0.25% or 0.5% of the value of the fund's security transactions. But you will have a hard time finding one that will tell you about the price concessions it had to make, which could probably only be verified by checking back to see what price ranges were available on the date of each trade.

Both the brokerage commissions and the price concessions are charged to you and the other fund shareholders, and they can add up to huge amounts, particularly if the fund does a lot of in-and-out trading.

Portfolio Turnover Rate: It Can Cost You Plenty, but Your Fund Doesn't Tell You How Much

How much trading your fund does is shown in the prospectus in a table headed Per Share Income and Capital Changes. Look for the line that says Portfolio Turnover Rate.

The turnover rate is the rate at which the fund buys and sells its holdings. A 100% rate would amount to all the fund's stocks being sold and replaced during the year. A 200% rate indicates the stocks were held on average for a period of only six months before the fund sold them. A fund with a 25% turnover rate holds its stocks for an average period of four years.

The amount of buying and selling some fund managers do in one year is little short of astounding. Some turn over their entire portfolio three or four times in a period of twelve short months. This 300% to 400% churning of stocks could indicate a portfolio manager who doesn't know his own mind or who is constantly trying to make a fast buck with your money. If the fund management is linked to a brokerage firm—some funds are owned by brokerage firms—it could indicate a policy of maximizing brokerage commissions.

In any event the portfolio turnover rate, like industry statistics in the Soviet Union's five-year plans, is invariably expressed in percentages. If you want hard figures in dollars and cents, you will have to estimate them yourself, but you will usually not have enough data available to do that with any accuracy. If you did find out, in actual dollars and cents, how much money a fund is spending on brokerage commissions (remember that this is probably understating the total because of unreported price concessions), you might lose your appetite for buying it. In any event, do not buy any fund without checking the prospectus for its portfolio turnover rate in the past five years. And do not buy it at all if the turnover rate is consistently high year after year, say, more than 80%.

Overall Fund Expenses: Add Them Up— They Cost You a Bundle

All these little percentages that add to a fund's cost may not seem like much individually if they are considered one at a time. But they add up relentlessly, and the damage they can do to you over the years piles up until it can almost cut your investment results in half. They can do even worse than that when combined with the ravages of inflation.

Consider this example. Over the past half century or so, stocks have averaged about a 9% yearly growth rate. Suppose you buy a fund which over the years will provide you with precisely that rate of return before expenses, so that after twenty-five years you'll have a nice little fund for your retirement. You invest $1,000 a year and reinvest all dividends.

Now, if the fund charged you no expenses at all, at the end of twenty-five years your investment would be worth $92,324.

If it nicked you for 1% in yearly expenses, so that your yield came down to 8%, you would end up with only $78,954.

If the fund hits you for 2% in yearly expenses, your net yield is down to 7% and your nest egg is worth only $67,676.

If you get slugged with 3% in yearly expenses, you are down to 6% net yield and your retirement fund is now worth only $58,156.

You get mugged with 4% yearly expenses—it can happen—your net income is only 5% and your retirement fund is reduced to a measly $50,113.

So the $64,000 question is: which would you rather have, $92,324 or $50,113?

As they say in Scotland, "Many a mickle makes a muckle."

Incidentally, the average U.S. inflation rate over the past half century was about 3% a year, so that a 9% yield on stocks would be reduced in real terms to only 6%. You might want to refigure the above calculations on that basis, particularly the last one, where your 5% net yield would be cut down to 1%.

Taxes Take Another Cut

If the impact of inflation can leave your mutual fund investment floundering in the surf, the thrust of taxes can push your head right under water—and most certainly will do so if your fund has a high expense ratio. The Tax Reform Act of 1986 made sure of this by restricting investment-related expenses as tax deductions for individual do-it-yourself investors. Unless they exceed 2% of your income, no more deductions for your home computer's financial software. Nor for the fees you pay your personal investment adviser. By the lawmaker's logic, if it's bad for the individual investor who buys stocks on his own, why should it be good for the mutual fund investor? So, to even the misery out for everybody, the new law says fund expenses are disallowed too.

Under the previous law, advisory fees and other mutual fund expenses were deducted from fund assets before taxable dividends were figured out for shareholders. No longer. Now your taxes are figured on the fund's gross income, a large part of which is soaked up by the fund's expenses and never even gets to you. In extreme cases, where the fund dividend is small and its expense ratio is high, the tax could amount to more than 100% of your dividend.

As a rule of thumb, this is going to happen to you if you are taxed at the top 28% rate and the fund's expenses amount to more than 72% of the fund's gross income.

Check these figures in your fund's annual report. According to the Investment Company Institute the tax bite won't amount to much on average. It estimates that the investor with about $10,000 in a fund that spends 0.5% to 1% of assets on annual expenses, which as we have seen is way below the average fund's expense ratio, will pay only an extra $20 or so in taxes every year. But if you have low income—say, from an aggressive growth fund that buys low-yielding stocks—and the high fund expenses that aggressive growth funds usually accumulate, you will have a major tax drain on your investment. The tax laws are simply compounding the disadvantages of funds that run high expense ratios. One more reason to stay away from them.

Choosing a Fund

So what is the bottom line of all this? How do you go about selecting a mutual fund that is likely to do well for you?

The plethora of funds before you is positively bewildering. The 2,000 funds available include growth funds, aggressive growth funds, leveraged growth funds, income funds, high-yield funds, balanced funds, index funds, dual-purpose funds, speculative funds, conservative funds, capital appreciation funds, money market funds, bond funds, convertible bond funds, municipal bond funds, tax-exempt funds, specialty funds, gold funds, high-technology funds, option funds, small-company funds, corporate-giant funds, socially aware funds, over-the-counter stock funds, special situations funds, global stock funds, medical technology funds, Canadian and Far Eastern stock funds, natural resource stock funds, precious metals stock funds, countercyclical funds, Ginnie Mae funds, biotechnology stock funds, electronics stock funds, utility stock funds, energy stock funds, food stock funds, financial stock funds, health stock funds, leisure stock funds, transportation stock funds, chemical, computer, defense, life insurance, property insurance, retail, savings and loan, computer software, and telecommunications stock funds. . . .

And on and on until your head spins.

So how do you choose amid all this welter of competing mutual fund companies, some of which have whole stables of funds, figuring that if they can't snare you with one they'll hook you with another?

First, by clearing all this confusion out of your head.

Let's take this one step at a time.

(We are assuming here that you are an absolute greenhorn in the mutual fund jungle and need absolutely everything explained to you. If you are a more sophisticated and battle-hardened veteran, please skip over the elementary explanations. You will also have to assume, unfortunately, that the authors of this book have a crystal ball that is no better than yours. We don't know how well gold funds are going to do in the next five years. We don't know if biotechnology funds are going to do better or worse than computer stock funds. We don't know if you will make more money in foreign stock funds than you will in funds that invest only in American corporations. We suspect that nobody, not even the oracle at Delphi, could give you the answers to these questions. The future is where it has always been, in the lap of the gods. So if you want to invest in the Intergalactic Exploration Fund, may the Force be with you. You will have to generate your own hologram of the future. But once you do that, you will have to come back to earth and see what is available in the real world here and now to make your dream a reality.)

So here we are. First, we have a universe of 2,000 funds to choose from. Now, the very last thing you want is an investment you can't readily get a quote on. You don't need to check the price of your mutual fund every day, but still you must have some way of knowing what your investment is worth at reasonably frequent intervals.

Get a copy of the *Wall Street Journal,* turn to the second section of the paper and look for the list of mutual fund quotations. If a fund is not on this list, then don't buy it. The *Journal* has the most comprehensive financial information available in the general American press, and if you don't find the fund quoted here then you probably won't find it quoted anywhere else. So ignore the blandishments of salesmen and advertisements for all those new funds that are springing up like mushrooms every day. You would have to telephone the fund itself for a quote, and you obviously don't want to do that.

You have now reduced the number of funds available to about 1,100, which is approximately the number quoted daily in the *Wall Street Journal* and most major American newspapers. Your local paper may have a shorter list.

The mutual funds are quoted something like this (we are going to use fictitious names because we don't want any arguments with disgruntled fund managers who might feel slighted by some of our comments):

Mutual Fund Quotations Monday Nov. 5, 1987			
	NAV	Offer Price	NAV Change
ABC Fund	$ 9.56	$10.45	−.02
DEF Fund	$13.58	$14.84	+.05
FUZZ Fund	$11.01	$11.56	+.01
RARA Fund	$10.62	$11.09	−.06
ZIP Fund	$21.65	NL	+.10
XYZ Fund	$ 8.08	NL	+.01

NAV means "net asset value." It is the true, honest-to-goodness value of one share (basically, the total value of all the different company stocks the fund holds, divided by the number of fund shares outstanding). ABC Fund, for example, is worth $9.56 per share. But that is not the price you will pay if you buy the ABC Fund. You are going to be charged the offer price, $10.45. The difference between $9.56 and $10.45 is 89 cents, and this is the amount that is going into the pocket of the salesperson who sells you the ABC Fund. The 89 cents—8.5% of your investment, or rather 9.3% if you figure it properly—is known as the load. For ABC Fund is a load fund. As you can easily tell from the figures, DEF Fund is a load fund, too. They both have salespeople who will eagerly and persistently pressure you to buy.

The FUZZ Fund has a smaller difference between the NAV price and its offer price. This is a low-load fund. The sales commission you are going to pay here is only 55 cents, or about 5% of your investment. The RARA Fund is another low-load, as you can tell by the narrow spread between the $10.62 NAV and the $11.09 Offer Price.

ZIP Fund has only one figure quoted, $21.65. This is its true value. It is also the price you will pay if you buy it, for the letters NL mean that it is a no-load fund. You will not be hit for any sales commission when you buy this fund, nor when you buy XYZ Fund, another no-load. Nor will any salespeople call on you because these funds have none.

Incidentally, the plus and minus figures to the right of the table mean that ZIP Fund closed Monday, November 5, with a 10-cent gain from the previous Friday's close. XYZ Fund closed with a 1-cent gain.

The advantage of buying ZIP or XYZ Fund is so obvious that we are not going to belabor the point any further. Any investment you make in ABC or DEF Fund is going to be 8.5% behind from the word go, and the chances are, it is never going to catch up because there is no reason to suppose that the people who run load funds are any sharper, wiser, brighter, more competent, or better clairvoyants than those who run no-load funds.

The low-load funds FUZZ and RARA are a somewhat better deal than the loads, but they still set you back three, four, or five percentage points at the start, and they are probably not going to catch up with the no-loads either.

So scratch all the load and low-load funds off your list. This gets rid of about half of all the funds quoted in the *Wall Street Journal.*

We are now down to somewhat more than 500 funds that are worth considering. These are the funds where your eye catches the magic letters NL as it sweeps down the columns of figures in the *Wall Street Journal.*

But do not assume that NL gives a fund an automatic seal of approval or that it is a ticket to Investors' Paradise. It doesn't and it isn't. There are still lots of nasty surprises in the NL columns.

One of these is the letter r next to a fund's name, which as you see from the explanation at the foot of the table, means this fund "may charge a redemption fee." This fee might be as much as 5% or 6%. It turns out that one of our no-loads, ZIP Fund, is one of these back-end specialists. This strikes us as a rather sneaky way of doing business so we throw out ZIP Fund and all its fellow back-loaders with the r designation. This has whittled down our list by about another sixty funds, some of which, as noted earlier in this chapter, slip through the net into the newspaper without being branded with that telltale r.

At this point you are going to need more information than the list of quotations in a daily newspaper is going to give you. Some useful sources are *Your Guide to Mutual Funds,* published annually and sold for $2 by the No-Load Mutual Fund Association (11 Penn Plaza, Suite 2204, New York, NY 10001); the *Individual Investor's Guide to No-Load Mutual Funds,* published annually by the American Association of Individual Investors, 612 N. Michigan Avenue, Chicago, IL 60611; and the *Handbook for No-Load Investors Annual,* published by the No-Load Investor, P.O. Box 283, Hastings on Hudson, NY 10706. Lipper Analytical Securities Corporation, 74 Trinity Place, New York, NY 10006, publishes a quarterly statistical report on more than 1,000 mutual funds. *Forbes* magazine also publishes a useful statistical survey of mutual funds in one of its biweekly September editions every year, while *Barron's* magazine runs the Lipper survey of funds every three months.

The first thing we find out on digging into this material is that some of the remaining funds on our list are 12b-1 funds. They are not eager to advertise this fact, however, and some of their prospectuses refer to the 12b-1 merely as "the Plan" or "the Distribution Plan." The 12b-1 means these funds are entitled to spend whatever they think is necessary to push the sales of the fund, and you and the other shareholders are going to pay for their advertising and promotion. They build up their business and you pay for it, year after year. *Chutzpah* could hardly go any further. And what do we find hidden deep in the prospectus of the ZIP Fund? "Rule 12b-1 permits a mutual fund to bear expenses of promoting the sale of its shares, including the cost of printing and

113

mailing prospectuses to other than current shareholders, if done pursuant to a plan that satisfies the requirements of the Rule. The Fund has adopted a 12b-1 Plan that permits the Fund to bear such costs. The Plan also authorizes the Fund to pay all brokerage commissions and advisory fees to the extent that those payments might be considered direct or indirect payment of sales promotion expenses by the Fund." The Fund, in case you hadn't noticed while digesting all this gobbledygook, is you.

There is only one fate these 12b-1 pirates deserve: walk the plank and then the old heave-ho.

The number of survivors among our no-loads is shrinking steadily, but as the Roman general said while decimating his mutinous legion "Nondum vos ad nihil confeci milites"—"I ain't through with you yet, men."

The next item to investigate is the expense ratio, which includes management and advisory fees. Our old friend ZIP Fund, we are curious to note, has an expense ratio that has varied in the past five years between 3.31% and 4.33% of net assets. It is going to have to do awfully well in the stock market before it makes any money for you at that rate—particularly when those expenses are passed on to you under the tax reform law.

Now, before we decide how many of these high spenders we are going to eject from our list, we have to have some idea of what a reasonable expense ratio is. As a benchmark, let's take a fund with an outstandingly low ratio, let us say the Vanguard Index Trust, with its yearly range of 0.27% to 0.42% over the past five years. One reason for this low ratio is that the fund makes no effort to beat the market or pick its own stocks and so has no need for any expensive investment advisers. It simply duplicates Standard & Poor's 500 Stock index by buying the stocks that make up this average. Not exactly a chimpanzee throwing darts at the stock lists, but still an essentially brainless activity. This fund, by design, will never do much worse than the general market, nor will it do appreciably better.

The other funds all try to be clever and beat the market, most of them with a notable lack of success, as we have noted. Nevertheless, let us give them the benefit of the doubt and concede that they do permit us at least some hope of an outstanding performance, and so deserve an extra allowance for their efforts—shall we say an extra 0.5% to 0.75% a year in the expense ratio? This would add up to a little over 1%, and as the average fund's ratio is about 1.1%, let us say that any fund with an expense ratio of 1.1% a year or less is acceptable. So out go all the others with ratios of more than 1.1%.

There are big gaps in the ranks now, but the legion faces one last decimation. The final test is the matter of transaction costs—the portfolio turnover rate.

Our old acquaintance XYZ Fund, as it happens, has had a yearly turnover rate ranging from 100% to 260% in the past five years. In other words it has made from one to two and a half complete changes in the stocks it owns every twelve months. This is surely not reasonable. But what is reasonable? Once again, let us take the Vanguard Index Trust as our benchmark. Simply in order to keep its portfolio in line with the S&P index (which means that every stock has to be owned in the same proportion as it figures in the index, more for the big companies, less for the small) the Vanguard Trust has had a portfolio turnover ranging from 11% to 39% a year. Let us give our fund managers some extra leeway for their clever market maneuvers and allow that a turnover rate twice as high as that, say 80%, is acceptable behavior.

The Bottom Line

Now, how do we apply this expense-cutting philosophy in our selection of mutual funds? Suppose we take the list of funds quoted in the *Wall Street Journal* and then exclude from our consideration (1) all load funds, (2) all low-load funds, (3) all back-end load funds, (4) all no-load funds with expense ratios that ran consistently above 1.1% a year over the past five years, (5) all funds with a portfolio turnover rate persistently higher than 80% a year over the past five years, and (6) all 12b-1 funds.

How would we have done in recent years if we had applied these penny-pinching rules? To judge by a number of independent surveys, unusually well.

To take points 1, 2, and 3 all in one bunch, suppose we had thrown out all the various types of load funds and concentrated on the no-loads. In its July 1985 issue, *Consumer Reports* magazine published a study of 289 mutual funds and rated them according to their performance over the five-year period 1980–1984. So as to reflect the experience of the average fund investor who puts money into his mutual fund whenever he can rather than all in one big lump sum, *Consumer Reports* assumed that the investor put $2,000 a year into each fund. It also deducted the sales commission he had to pay. Twenty-three of the top thirty funds in the *Consumer Reports* survey were no-loads.

To take point 4, the matter of expense ratios, the annual survey of mutual funds published by *Forbes* magazine in September 1986 is highly illuminating. *Forbes* rated the performance of more than 800 funds of all types over the 9¾-year period from September 1976 to June 1986, which covered three complete bear and bull market cycles. It assumed that the investor made a single investment of $10,000 at the beginning of the period. *Forbes* singled out twenty-three funds that turned in an outstanding performance: they boosted the initial $10,000 investment into amounts ranging from $50,420 to $151,684. These figures take into account any sales loads and taxes a well-to-do investor would have had to pay. Of these twenty-three star performers, twenty had expense ratios lower than our limit of 1.1%. None of the other three had ratios higher than 1.30%.

And now to wrap up our conclusions, let us consider

the funds that met all our criteria, 1 through 6: no load of any kind, low expense ratios and portfolio turnovers, and no 12b-1 plan.

These funds are to be found in a survey made in the 1986 *Individual Investor's Guide to No-Load Mutual Funds*. The *Guide*, published by the American Association of Individual Investors, included all the no-load funds publicly quoted in the financial press in December 1985—basically the no-loads listed in the *Wall Street Journal* table, which number more than 400. The *Guide* excluded all the no-load funds that were closed to new investors, that had unusually high minimum deposits so as to exclude small investors, that were restricted to special groups of investors, or that failed to provide information. This brought the list down to 286, of which only sixty-five satisfy all our six investment criteria.

The *Guide* then ranked the fifty top-performing no-loads over the 1981–1985 period. Statistically, every one of the 286 funds in the survey thus had about a one-in-six chance of making the top fifty. However, it turns out that twenty-four of our select group of sixty-five (this is our selection, by the way, and is not included in the *Guide* survey) are in the top fifty. So by insisting on low expenses, low portfolio turnover, and no 12b-1 plan, we have shortened the odds for ourselves from one in six to better than one in three.

This is not all, however. Not only do twenty-four of the top fifty meet all our criteria. Of the remaining twenty-six star performers, no less than twenty-one satisfy at least the low expense ratio or else the low portfolio turnover requirement. Only five of the fifty fail to pass our penny-pinching tests—and mostly they fail only by a whisker.

Listed below are the *Guide*'s top-rated no-loads (note that five of them have 12b-1 plans), plus the funds in the survey that satisfy all our criteria, 1 through 6, and so would seem to have a good chance of climbing into the top fifty in the future:

Acorn
American Leaders (Liberty)
Babson Bond Trust
Boston Capital Growth Appreciation (12b-1)
Century Shares Trust
Columbia Growth (12b-1)
Copley Tax-Managed
Dodge & Cox Balanced
Dodge & Cox Stock
Dreyfus A Bonds Plus
Dreyfus Growth Opportunity
Dreyfus Special Income
Dreyfus Third Century
Energy Fund
Evergreen
Evergreen Total Return
Fidelity Discoverer
Fidelity Fund
Fidelity High Income
Fidelity Puritan
Fidelity Thrift
Fidelity Trend
Financial Industrial Income
Founders Mutual (12b-1)
Fund for U.S. Government Securities
Growth Industry Shares
Guardian Mutual
Istel
Ivy Growth (12b-1)
Janus (12b-1)
Lehman Capital
Lehman Investors
Lehman Opportunity
Loomis Sayles Capital Development
Loomis Sayles Mutual
Nicholas
Nicholas Income
North Star Bond

North Star Regional
North Star Stock
Northeast Investors Trust
Partners
Penn Square Mutual
Quest for Value
T. Rowe Price Growth
T. Rowe Price International
T. Rowe Price New Era
T. Rowe Price New Horizons
Safeco Equity
Safeco Income
Scudder Capital Growth
Scudder Growth & Income
Scudder International
Selected American Shares
Smith Barney Equity
Steinroe & Farnham Capital Opportunities
Steinroe Special
Tudor
Twentieth Century Select
Unified Growth
Unified Income
Unified Mutual Shares
United Services Gold Shares
USAA Growth
USAA Income
Value Line Income
Value Line Special Situations
Vanguard GNMA
Vanguard High Yield Bond
Vanguard Index Trust
Vanguard Investment Grade Bond
Vanguard Trustee Commingled U.S. Portfolio
Vanguard W.L. Morgan Growth
Vanguard Wellesley
Vanguard Wellington

Babson Tax Free Income L
Babson Tax Free Income S
Dreyfus Tax-Exempt
Federated Tax-Free Income
Fidelity High Yield Municipals
Kentucky Tax-Free Income
Nuveen Municipal
Selected Tax-Exempt
Steinroe Tax-Exempt

This group of less than 100 no-load funds represents less than 10% of all the funds listed in the *Wall Street Journal*, and less than 5% of all the American funds in existence. Yet the funds on this list show up in disproportionate numbers in all the surveys mentioned above. They account for seven of the top twenty-three funds in the *Forbes* September 1986 survey, for example. They account for twelve of the top thirty in the 1985 *Consumer Reports* survey. They also account for six of the top twenty-five in the ten-year Lipper survey of December 31, 1986. They account for eight of the thirty top total return funds in the fall 1986 three-year performance survey published by *Money* magazine, and four of the top twenty growth funds in the same three-year *Money* magazine survey.

Many of these surveys, it might be noted in passing (the *Forbes* ranking of the top twenty-three funds is one notable exception to this), are less than perfect guides to the individual investor looking for a good mutual fund, because they compare apples with oranges. They do not take into account the fact that load funds skim 9.3% of your money off the top, and they are thus strongly biased against the no-load funds. If they were not so biased, the results of the surveys cited above would have favored our selected list of top-performing funds even more emphatically than they do. The surveys mostly tell you how much a $10,000 investment grew to, but make no allowance for sales charges. It is crucial to make this allowance, because a load fund would put only $9,150 of your money to work as against the full $10,000 by a no-load fund. The method used by most surveys compares the performance of one fund with another fairly enough, but does not reflect the results you achieve as an individual investor—and that is what counts for you.

Evidently our method of selecting mutual funds on the basis of their investment expenses, sales charges, and other costs gets some pretty solid statistical confirmation in the actual results in recent years. This should not really come as any great surprise to anyone, however. It stands to reason that if you cut your costs of doing business you are going to get better results, whatever business you are in.

This is not to say that you should completely and categorically exclude any funds that are not on our list. Obviously, other funds make it into the top twenty-five too, and there is usually a good reason for this. The main one is, of course, that there is a craze for health stocks or whatever in the stock market, economic conditions over the past few years have been favorable to health stocks, and the fund just happens to specialize in health stocks.

Another, less frequent, reason might be that the fund has a superduper stock-picker. There are a few such people around—a very few—who consistently beat the market over the years. One is John Templeton, whose funds have consistently outperformed the competition. If you had bought his Templeton Growth Fund in 1955, your $10,000 investment would have grown with reinvested dividends to $794,610 in 1986. Another is Peter Lynch of Fidelity Magellan, who has regularly turned in a superior performance from the time his fund had a $20-million portfolio ten years ago to its present status as the world's biggest equity mutual fund, with more than $7 billion in assets.

Another thing. The list of ninety funds given above

is not written forever in granite. You will have to update it when the time comes for you to invest, and the books and publications mentioned in this chapter should provide you with the data you need to do so.

You may not have the time or inclination to do all the research detailed above. And in fact you don't really need to. All you have to do is ask yourself a few simple questions once you have the fund's prospectus in your hands, and before you write out that first check:

1. Does this no-load fund have an expense ratio higher than 1.1%?
2. Does it consistently have a portfolio turnover of more than 80% a year?
3. Is it a 12b-1 fund?

If the answer to all three is yes, then don't buy it unless it has an exceptionally distinguished record in the past five, ten, or fifteen years, such as ranking in the top ten, twenty, or fifty mutual funds in the country.

But we still think the main question to ask about any fund—indeed about any stock market investment—is this: would it fly on a Monday morning after the minister and the church finance committee have finished examining its expenses?

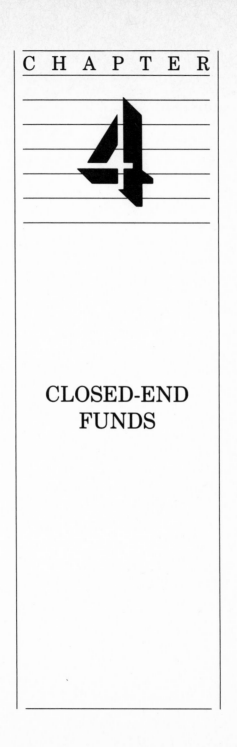

CHAPTER

4

CLOSED-END FUNDS

Bargains to Buy at a Discount, Bargains to Sell at a Premium

Suppose there were a special type of investment fund that, with time and patience, you could buy at a discount of 30% or more and then sell at a premium of 20% or better some years later. Wouldn't this beat investing in mutual funds? Thirty percent off certainly beats the 8.5% sales charge on a load mutual fund when you are buying. And not even a no-load can offer you a 20% premium when the time comes for you to sell.

The fact is, there are such funds. And yet, strangely enough, they are ignored by the vast majority of investors. One such fund is Niagara Share Corporation, which in the past thirty-one years has traded at a discount of as much as 34% (that is to say, you could buy it at 34% less than the total value of all the individual stocks in its portfolio), in June 1956, and at a premium as high as 21%, in March 1970.

There are other funds of this particular type, about 100 of them in the United States, plus several hundred more in Great Britain and other countries. They are called closed-end funds or publicly traded funds. Some of the most actively traded American funds are listed below. The data are compiled weekly by the Association of Publicly Traded Investment Funds and provided to the press through J. W. Seligman Inc. You will find the list with the latest prices in the Monday edition of the *Wall Street Journal* and the *New York Times*, in *Barron's* weekly financial magazine, and in other publications under the headings Publicly Traded Funds or Closed-End Stock Funds.

On this particular table, which carries prices of January 9, 1987, you will note that Niagara Share Corp. had a net asset value of $17.39 a share but was trading in stock exchange dealings at only 15⅝, a discount of 10.1%. Meanwhile Tri-Continental shares had a net asset value of $30.49 a share but were selling at 32⅜, a premium of 6.2%.

You will observe even more extreme examples on this table: Korea Fund selling at a 29% premium and ASA Ltd. trading at a 53.5% discount.

If your bargain hunter's nose smells out double profit-making potential here—first buying these funds at a discount and then selling them at a premium—your nose is right on the money. The fund that is selling at a discount this year may be selling at a premium next year, and vice versa.

You have a double-barreled profit-making opportunity here that no mutual fund can ever offer you. And yet the vast majority of investors ignore these closed-end funds. The nearly 2,000 mutual funds outnumber them by about twenty to one. Mutual funds had total assets of more than $700 billion in 1987 while closed-end funds had a relatively meager $15 billion.

Diversified Common Stock Funds			
	N.A. Value	Stock Price	% Diff.
Adams Express	20.80	21⅜	+ 2.8
Baker Fentress	54.48	46	−15.6
Equity Guard	b9.78	9	− 8.0
Gem II Cap	b15.96	14¾	− 7.6
Gem II Inc	b9.74	14⅝	+50.2
Gen'l Amer Inv	21.06	19¼	− 8.6
GlobalGr Cap	10.04	9⅜	− 6.6
GlobalBR-Inc	9.41	11¼	+19.6
GSO Trust	9.72	8⅞	− 8.7
Lehman	16.80	16½	− 1.8
Lbty All-Star	10.63	9⅝	− 9.5
Niagara Share	17.39	15⅝	−10.1
Royce Value	9.64	10¾	+11.5
Schafer Valu	9.28	9	− 3.0
Source	40.20	43⅛	+ 7
Tri-Continental	30.49	32⅜	+ 6.2
Worldwd Val	18.97	17	−10.4
ZweigFund	9.81	9⅝	− 1.9

In the brokerage community the situation is even more one-sided. There are thousands of stock brokerage firms but only one of them, Thomas J. Herzfeld & Co., with its affiliated investment advisory firm, Thomas J. Herzfeld Advisors Inc. of Miami, specializes exclusively in closed-end funds.

And yet "the risk-reward relationship in trading closed-end funds represents the best opportunity the stock market has to offer," says Herzfeld.

So what exactly is a closed-end fund? And why is it so overlooked? And can you really make money out of it, even if most other investors don't even try? And how exactly do you go about making money out of it?

It may well be worth your efforts to find out. To many investors these funds appear complicated and arcane.

126

Specialized Equity and Convertible Funds

	N.A. Value	Stock Price	% Diff.
Amer Cap Cv	a28.33	33½	+18.2
ASA	bc84.35	39⅜	−53.3
Bancroft Conv	26.60	28⅛	+ 5.7
Castle Conv	28.26	28⅝	+ 1.3
CenFdCanada	b5.77	5⅜	− 6.9
Central Sec	13.99	13	− 7.1
Claremont	52.12	59	+13.2
CLAS	z	z	z
CLAS PFD	z	z	z
Cypress Fd	9.90	9⅝	− 2.8
Ellsworth Cv	9.71	9¼	− 4.7
EmgMdTech	b15.14	13⅞	− 8.4
Engex	20.41	20	− 2.0
1st Australia	11.93	9⅞	−17.2
Fst Fn Fd	9.15	7⅞	−13.9
Gabelli E	9.88	9⅜	− 5.1
France Fd	b15.92	11½	−27.8
Germany Fd	10.65	10⅜	− 2.6
Italy Fd	b14.32	10¾	−24.9
Japan Fund	20.65	15⅝	−24.3
Korea Fund	27.72	35¾	+29.0
Mexico	b5.91	4	−3.23
MI Cv-Inc	9.36	13⅝	+46.0
ML Cv-Cap	11.80	7¼	−39.0
Pete & Res	29.78	32⅛	+ 7.9
PilREg	9.74	8⅞	− 8.9
Reg Finl/Shs	8.93	8⅛	− 9.0
Scandinavia	b9.92	8⅝	− 1.3
Z-Seven	d17.47	22½	+28.8

They look on their premiums and discounts with incomprehension and suspicion.

Perhaps as a result of this, "the closed-end fund discount is the most overlooked and misunderstood concept in the modern stock market," says Herzfeld. "It is also the modern stock market's greatest value. It gives investors an opportunity to buy entire portfolios of stocks at 70 and 80 cents on the dollar. Closed-end funds might be overlooked and ignored by the Wall Street herd, but not by the intelligent investor."

Herzfeld is of course pushing his own wares, which have their drawbacks, just like any other investment, and you will most certainly not make money out of them until you understand what they are and how they work.

As Benjamin Graham, one of Wall Street's most revered gurus, once said, "The price discount of these companies may be viewed as an expensive monument erected to the inertia and stupidity of stockholders."

The discount "has cost owners of these businesses countless millions of dollars," said Graham, the mentor of some of Wall Street's most successful professional investment managers, "yet it has been totally unnecessary. It could have been terminated at any time by the mere passing of a resolution at a stockholders' meeting. Yet the matter never seems to have been brought up for discussion." (In recent years, however, the managements of some closed-end funds have taken steps to ensure that such resolutions are difficult to introduce and impossible to pass.)

The amount of money involved here is certainly worth going for. Herzfeld estimates that in recent years the discounts on all the closed-end funds added together would come to more than $1 billion in the United States, and $8 billion globally. There is money to be made, but evidently there are right ways and wrong ways to invest in closed-end funds. What can be expected to work, basically, is the philosophy that is so relentlessly expounded throughout this book: cut your investment costs to the bone—which in this case means buying at the greatest possible discount—and then sell at the greatest possible premium. Easy enough to state. But in practice as in everything else, from cooking a small fish to gov-

erning a great empire, there are a number of things you
need to know first.

Open-End and Closed-End: What's the Difference?

First of all, what is the difference between a closed-end,
or publicly traded, fund and an open-end, or mutual, fund?
And how does it come about that the closed-end may sell
at a discount or a premium while the mutual fund
doesn't?

Let's start with the mutual fund. The first thing to
keep in mind is that when you buy or sell shares in a
mutual fund you are always dealing directly with the
fund itself, not with another investor. And in every case,
whether buying or selling, the price is set by the fund:
the price is the net asset value of the fund at the time
of the transaction (plus a sales commission if you are
spendthrift enough to buy a load fund). This means that
the fund adds up the value of the various stocks in its
portfolio daily—which comes, let us say, to $100 mil-
lion—and then divides this by the number of shares outstanding. If there are 10 million shares outstanding, then
the net asset value will be $10 per share ($100 million
divided by 10 million). And that is the price you will
receive when you sell. It is also the price you will pay
when you buy a no-load fund ($10.85 if you buy shares
in a load fund).

The next thing to remember is that the number of
shares in a mutual fund is not a fixed amount. If you
buy 20,000 shares, for example, then the 10,000,000-share
total mentioned above will rise to 10,020,000. And if your
rich Great Aunt Agatha should sell 500,000 shares that
same day, then the total would shrink to 9,520,000.

The mutual fund is thus constantly issuing new
shares and buying back its old shares. Which is precisely why it is called an open-end fund.

The closed-end fund doesn't do this. It issues, let us say, 15 million shares when the fund is launched in 1886 or 1986 or whichever year it goes into business, and this amount never varies for years at a time, unless a new issue is specifically authorized by its stockholders. As new shares are not being continually issued, it is known as a closed-end fund.

This brings us to the next major difference between the mutual fund and the closed-end fund. Mutual funds are not traded on stock exchanges because they deal directly with the public. Closed-end funds, however, do not stand ready to buy or sell their shares directly to investors at a specified price, so their shares are traded in the stock market. You trade them with other investors just as you do with IBM or AT&T or any other company share. You look up the latest price in your newspaper's listings of New York Stock Exchange, American Stock Exchange, or over-the-counter quotations, and if you like what you see you place your buy or sell order through your stockbroker. How many buyers or sellers your broker will find out there depends on each individual fund: some funds are heavily traded, while others may have rather thin markets.

Anyway, when you buy or sell a closed-end fund, you are buying or selling to another investor; you are not dealing with the fund itself. And this is where the discount and the premium both come in, because the investors you are going to trade with may be willing to pay a premium over net asset value if they are optimistic about the fund's outlook. Or they may be willing to buy the fund only at a discount if they don't think much of its prospects.

This optimism or pessimism may go to wild extremes. In the table of quotations given above, it is obvious that investors in general were wildly optimistic about Korea Fund since they had bid the share up to a 29% premium. They were even more gloomy about ASA

Ltd. than they were optimistic about Korea Fund, driving it down to a 53.3% discount.

Now, strange as it may seem, it is possible that some unsophisticated investors in Korea Fund may not even have realized that they were paying such a huge premium for their shares. This is because they look up the daily stock market quote in their newspaper, which lists the market price only—35¾ for Korea Fund on this particular date—and they do not bother to check the net asset value, which appears only once a week, as we noted above, in that separate little item in the financial press.

So if you want to get yourself off the sucker list right now, rule number one is: never buy or sell a closed-end fund without first checking to see whether it is trading at a premium or at a discount.

The next step is to figure out why the fund is selling at a premium or a discount, and discover whether there is any sort of predictable pattern to its price behavior from which one could profit.

One curious feature of closed-end funds that immediately leaps to mind is that most of them sell at a discount most of the time. Niagara Share Corp., for instance, traded at a discount at year-end in seventeen of the last twenty-five years and at a premium in only eight years. The average discount on all United States closed-end funds ranged between 20% and 28% in the years 1974 to 1980. Since then, the average discount has tended to narrow, sinking as low as 1% in 1984.

There are a number of reasons for the persistent, depressing discount that the closed-end funds seem unable to shake off, and these reasons also go far toward explaining the average investor's lack of interest in them.

When a customer comes looking for advice, brokerage firms almost invariably recommend a load mutual fund rather than a closed-end fund, for the very good reason that a customer who invests, say, $10,000 in the mutual fund will produce an $850 commission, while the client who buys the closed-end fund will produce only $100 or so in brokerage fees. Once he has bought the closed-end fund, moreover, the client is likely to sit on it for years and years. If he can't be persuaded to buy the load fund, the broker thinks, better then to steer him into some other stock where he is more likely to trade more actively in and out and keep his broker busy and well fed. Most big brokerage firms also have their own lists of recommended stocks, and the customer's man in that firm is usually reluctant to admit that the closed-end fund's portfolio strategy is better than his own firm's recommendations. He is also under pressure from his boss to push those recommended stocks.

Add to all this the plain old ignorance of some brokers. When Wall Street trainees are given their basic training courses, they are instructed in the ins and outs of all kinds of investments, from naked options to Ginnie Maes. "But about closed-end funds," says Herzfeld, "hardly a word is spoken. They seem not to exist. And if they do it is in a financial limbo."

Independent investment advisers also tend to ignore the closed-end funds. When some of them do show a brief interest, the closed-ends tend to rally, but Herzfeld notes that the interest "surfaces briefly and then fades completely, for months if not years. Since the 1930s there has been a pitiable amount of interest in them for any sustained length of time."

And then there are also the defects that any investment company of whatever type is liable to exhibit. Closed-end funds are just as likely as mutual funds to run up large operating expenses and to be operated by incompetent or misguided management. These factors lead to equally poor performance in both cases, but the closed-end fund offers at least this consolation: the shortcomings tend to be reflected by a widening discount in the fund's market price. You cannot say the same of a mutual fund.

It would be tedious to go through the whole penny-pinching strictures again, but it cannot be emphasized too strongly that everything we have said about mutual fund expenses applies in full and equal measure to the running expenses of closed-end funds. They too are required to state their operating expenses as a percentage of net assets in their annual reports. Check this figure before you can buy any closed-end fund. If it is consistently above 1% over the last few years, think twice before you buy any closed-end fund. If it is consistently above 1% over the last few years, think twice be-is persistently above, say, 80%, stay away from the fund—it is churning its portfolio, most probably to no useful purpose.

Herzfeld notes that "a fund drifting to a 10% discount may merely be compensating for 10% of operating expenses." This may well be so, but a mutual fund piling up similar expenses makes no such allowance for its own profligacy when you are buying its shares.

Whatever the cause of its poor performance, if a closed-end fund consistently achieves poorer results than the Dow Jones industrial average or Standard & Poor's index of 500 stocks, then investors will tend to pay less for it and it will decline to a discount. There is no reason to suppose that closed-end funds will be any more competently managed than mutual funds, and we have seen that mutual funds habitually underperform the market averages. So we may have a large part of the explanation for the perennial discount right there.

Another factor is marketing. Closed-end funds tend to be diffident about advertising, particularly when their shares are selling at a discount, which is difficult to explain to a skeptical and uninformed public. It does not help their sales effort either when their shares sell at a premium. Mutual funds tend to push their wares aggressively, particularly if they have 12b-1 plans and can make their shareholders pay for the advertising. Since they do so little to promote themselves, closed-end funds do not have 12b-1 plans.

And finally there is the discount itself, which quite logically induces the fear of an even larger discount. If an investor buys the fund at a 20% discount, what assurance does he have that it may not have dropped to a 30% discount when the time comes for him to sell? This alone would make anyone wary and reluctant to bet on closed-end funds.

Nevertheless, even Herzfeld, who has spent his entire working life dealing exclusively with closed-end funds, admits that "I have never seen a complete and accurate explanation of why closed-end funds sell at a discount."

The subject has been explored by closed-end fund economists and by academic researchers, but they too have failed to come up with a full, final, definitive explanation.

Eugene J. Pratt, director of research at Niagara Share Corporation, concluded in one study that closed-end fund shares "sell at a discount primarily because of lack of sales effort and public understanding."

A study by Morris Mendelson, professor of finance at the Wharton School at the University of Pennsylvania, concluded in 1977 after thirty-three pages of text and columns of sophisticated mathematical formulas that "only about half of the variance in the discount can be explained. . . . Few firm conclusions can be drawn from the statistics presented here. Certainly there is evidence to suggest that the market for closed-end companies is less than perfect."

"This study," Prof. Mendelson concluded, "suggests that an exploration of trading strategies might be fruitful."

And that is what we will now explore.

Trading Strategies

Let us start at the beginning, with the launching of a new closed-end fund. Some funds have been around for nearly a century, but new ones are always coming on the market—about thirty in 1986 alone—and the first rule of the game is to stay away from the new ones when they are first issued.

First of all, the new fund has not yet moved to a discount, so it is no great bargain. Second, the brokers who underwrite the issue are collecting a commission of about 7%, which means you are paying nearly as much of a sales commission as you would on a load mutual fund. Third, new closed-end funds are usually launched when there is a craze for the kind of stocks they plan to invest in: biotechnology companies, health-care stocks, foreign stocks, robotics, or whatever the current fad is. This is in fact the only time they can be successfully launched on the market, but by the time they come to market the craze for those particular stocks is likely to be near a peak and ready for a fall.

So we are going to concentrate on the established funds that have a verifiable track record extending over at least several years. We are going to limit ourselves to the funds that are listed weekly in such publications as *Barron's* and the *Wall Street Journal,* because they are the only ones where it is possible for us to keep constantly informed as to whether they are currently trading at a discount or at a premium. This is the one major piece of information that is indispensable for an intelligent investment decision on a closed-end fund.

The premium and the discount, which might add 50% to a fund's market price or subtract 50% from its purchase cost, are so overwhelmingly important that they have to be given first priority in selecting a closed-end fund. The factors that are so important in a mutual fund—the fund's expense ratio, its portfolio turnover rate (which are unlikely to exceed 10% between them), and even its performance against the market averages—are of only secondary importance in choosing a closed-end fund.

Now we are going to buy funds at the largest discount possible and sell them at the highest premium we can get. Let's spell out the advantages we expect to gain by this. They are considerable.

First, you get leverage. If the fund you buy is selling at a 30% discount, which as we have seen is by no means impossible or even all that unusual, you are buying $100 worth of stock for every $70 you invest. Suppose your fund shares have a net asset value of $10,000. Thanks to the discount, you bought them for $7,000 and thus spread your money over, say, fifty different companies in the fund's portfolio. If the portfolio goes up 10% in value that is a $1,000 gain, but a $1,000 gain on your $7,000 investment becomes a 14.3% gain.

Now consider the alternatives. You could have invested in those fifty companies one by one, but you would have paid the full $10,000 for them instead of $7,000. You would have fifty different investments of about $200 each, which would be prohibitively expensive in brokerage commissions.

You could also have invested on margin, putting up $7,000 yourself and borrowing the other $3,000 from your broker. But you would have had to pay the broker interest on the margin loan. The closed-end fund at a discount in effect gives you a margin loan for free.

Or you could have put your money into a mutual fund, which we will say owned exactly the same fifty shares as the closed-end fund. In that case your investment would have cost you the full $10,000 if it was a no-load fund—even more if it was a load fund.

The same argument applies to yields, and it is particularly important in the case of closed-end bond funds, which we will examine in detail further on. If you buy a fund at a 20% discount, you put up $8,000 but you get the dividends and interest on a $10,000 portfolio. If the fund is yielding 10%, that is a $1,000 yearly income. And a $1,000 yield on your $8,000 investment comes to 12.5%, not 10%.

When the fund moves up and starts trading at a premium, all these arguments shift into reverse. Your

$10,000 investment is then buying only an $8,000 port-folio and yielding a proportionately smaller income. When this happens you know that the time has come to sell out to investors less sophisticated than yourself, grab your profits, and run.

Now let's refine this a little further. The major danger you face with a closed-end fund is that even if you bought at a discount of 20% the discount may widen to say 30%. So you decide to buy only when the fund is selling at an excessive discount. The problem is, how do you know when the discount is excessive?

Like this, says Herzfeld: keep a file of the closed-end funds' prices and their discounts (we suggest you clip the weekly table). Then take the three widest discounts (let's say 30%, 32%, and 34%) at which the fund traded over the past year and average them (in our example the average is 32%). Next take the three narrowest discounts (say 20%, 21%, and 22%) and average them (in our example we average out at 21%).

Now, when the discount is greater than 32% you buy, and when it is less than 21% you sell.

Herzfeld has another, more complicated, strategy to take advantage of the fact that a closed-end fund's discount is constantly widening and narrowing over the years. However it involves more work, more time, and more research on charts, moving averages, and computer calculations—and considerably more active trading, thus adding to your investment costs. For further details you might read Herzfeld's book *The Investor's Guide to Closed-End Funds,* which you might find in your public library. It is also available through Thomas J. Herzfeld & Co. for $50 ($25 for subscribers to Herzfeld's research service, which costs $200 yearly for twelve monthly reports on closed-end funds).

Herzfeld (7800 Red Road, South Miami, FL 33143) deals in such sophisticated maneuvers as the Herzfeld Hedge, an arbitrage strategy that involves buying a closed-end fund and simultaneously establishing a short position in the listed options (this means buying a put option) of the main stocks in the fund's portfolio. If the fund goes up you make money on the fund, and if it goes down you make money on the options. At the very least, this strategy will limit your possible losses, and at its best it will make you a nice profit.

According to Herzfeld, closed-end funds move in a fairly predictable pattern with the ups and downs of the stock market: the discount tends to widen when the stock market is declining and investors are overcome by pessimism. The discount narrows or even disappears and turns into a premium when the stock market is rising and investors are carried away by their own optimism. This appears to make good sense psychologically.

What this means in fact is that closed-end funds tend to exaggerate market trends. They tend to sink too low in falling markets and then to overcompensate on the upside when the market rises again.

So who wants to invest in a closed-end fund when he knows that it will fall even further than most other stocks in the market? Either a fool or a smart investor. The fool buys when the stock market is enveloped in a rosy haze of optimism and the closed-end fund is selling at a premium, and then gets hurt when it sinks to a discount. The intelligent investor buys when pessimism is rampant and the closed-end fund is selling at a discount. He reaps his reward in trumps when the market turns up and his funds swing to a premium.

Herzfeld recommends this basic strategy: in bull markets buy undervalued funds, that is to say, funds selling at wide discounts. In bear markets sell the overvalued funds short, those at narrow discounts or even at premiums. His reasoning is that in the early stages of the bull market the closed-end funds are still selling at excessive discounts, reflecting the deep pessimism of the preceding bear market. As the market rises, the discount narrows and you do even better than the general market. And then when the bull market crests and sinks into the next bear market the closed-end funds are still reflecting the public's lingering bullishness with unusually small discounts or even premiums. If you sell the funds short at this point you will do better than the general market because the fund will (1) sink with the rest of the market, and (2) drop even further than that because of its widening discount.

According to Herzfeld there is also a seasonal pattern to closed-end funds. Discounts almost always widen toward the end of the year. This is because investors tend to sell funds in which they have a loss so as to offset any capital gains they may have realized in other securities.

"Quite often," says Herzfeld, "the funds tend to rebound in January, and the investor who made a tax-loss sale forfeits more by selling the fund than he gains in the tax savings."

In any case the moral seems clear: buy closed-end funds in November and December; sell them in January.

How much money can you expect to make by investing in closed-end funds in this way? Herzfeld's objective is 20% profit a year, but he hastens to add that there is no guarantee that he will achieve that.

When a Closed-End Closes Down

We started this part of the chapter with the birth of a fund. Let us end it with the death of a fund, noting in passing that it may be considerably more profitable to be in at the death than to be in at the birth.

It might have occurred to you that if you could buy up an entire closed-end fund at a 30% discount and sell off its assets you would have an instant 30% profit. Or that if you could convert the closed-end fund into a regular open-end, or mutual, fund, your share holdings would be immediately worth 30% more on being priced at net asset value. Both these things do come about occasionally, and they are something to watch out for with gleeful anticipation.

A number of closed-end funds have been converted into mutual funds: Boston Personal Property Trust in 1967, when it had been selling at a 20% discount; Consolidated Investment Trust that same year, also trading at a 20% discount at the time; and Dominick Fund in 1974, then at a 22% discount. In 1966 the M.A. Hanna Company was liquidated at $51 a share. It had been trading at $40, a 25% discount. Instant profits for everybody on the stockholder rolls when these closed-end funds were converted or liquidated. Another thirty or so closed-end funds have been wound up since 1980—from American Dual Vest to U.S. & Foreign Securities—at varying degrees of satisfaction for the shareholders.

Different Types of Closed-End Funds

You will note that the list of quotations of closed-end stock funds is divided into two sections: diversified common stock funds, and specialized equity and convertible funds. (Closed-end bond funds are listed in a separate table, which we will get to later.)

The time has come to examine these in detail. You will probably want to start with the diversified common stock funds since they do not require any narrowly specialized knowledge other than a general understanding of the stock market. A specialty fund such as Korea Fund or Japan Fund or Petroleum & Resources Fund demands at least a rudimentary comprehension of the particular angles involved in investing in a foreign country or in a particular economic sector such as the oil industry.

The diversified common stock funds are your basic, regulation-issue, general-purpose closed-end fund. Those that exist today include battle-scarred survivors of the Great Crash of 1929 and other assorted ups and downs of the stock market since then.

The pioneer in the field, the Boston Personal Property Trust, is gone but by no means dead. Created in 1893 as a closed-end fund, it was the first investment trust in the United States and survived in that form until 1967, when it was converted into a mutual fund—at a nice profit for its stockholders, as we have seen.

The closed-end funds reached their heyday in the 1920s, when hundreds of funds were formed and flourished until the stock market crash of 1929. Their experience in the crash then closely paralleled the experience of individual investors. Individuals investing heavily on margin were practically wiped out, and those who had not borrowed money to buy stock did relatively better.

According to the Securities and Exchange Commission, highly leveraged funds lost 95% of their value between 1929 and 1937, while the nonleveraged funds (those that did not borrow money to finance their stock purchases) were worth just under half what they were before the 1929 crash.

Tri-Continental—the biggest closed-end fund in existence today, with about $1 billion in assets—and others managed to survive, but the crash was just as devastating to closed-end funds in general as it was to the average American investor. The conservatively run funds tended to get tarred with the brush of the speculative highly leveraged funds that went under. The closed-end funds as a group never regained the glamour, the excitement, the reputation, and the status they enjoyed in the Roaring Twenties.

After 1929 practically all the growth in the investment company industry was in the open-end, or mutual, funds—a curious development since the open-end funds are, if anything, even more vulnerable to sudden market crashes than the closed-ends.

At the present time the ground rules for both open-end and closed-end funds are set by the Investment Company Act of 1940. The Act was intended to protect American investors from the disasters that befell them when the freewheeling days of the 1920s came crashing down. If you own shares in either a mutual fund or a closed-end fund, you can be fairly sure that you will not share the fate of the unsuspecting investors who put their money into the highly leveraged funds of the 1920s. If a fund is going to invest on margin it has to say so, and tell you to what extent it is going into hock, and you would be well advised to scan its prospectus for any mention of the word "margin." Nor can they perpetrate a favorite scam of the 1920s: distribute as dividends the profits of one-shot sales of securities without disclosing that these are just one-shot deals.

The diversified common stock funds on the weekly list require some comment because in some cases the classification is misleading. Gemini II Capital and Gemini II Income are in fact specialized funds even though they may have a diversified portfolio (the capital shares get all the capital gains, while the income shares get all the income from the fund's portfolio). The same setup applies to Global Growth & Income Fund (and to ML Convertible Fund, which appears among the specialized funds).

Niagara Share Corp. usually has a fairly substantial portion of its portfolio invested in foreign securities. Adams Express, Baker Fentress, General American Investors, Lehman, Source Capital, and Tri-Continental are the funds that come closest to giving a cross section of the U.S. market.

The expense ratios of all these funds tend to vary widely. Tri-Continental, thanks largely to its huge size, is relatively low. The newer and smaller funds tend to be higher.

142

New Funds

Let us hope this is not an omen of things to come, but for new closed-end funds 1986 was a banner year such as had not been seen since about 1926 or so when the Roaring Twenties were heading for the Great Crash of 1929. Nearly thirty new closed-end funds came onto the market in 1986, about $4 billion worth. Why in 1986? Probably for two main reasons: the stock market was soaring, and with the average discount on closed-end funds shrinking to a relatively small percentage, the promoters of these funds grabbed their chance. It is usually rather hard to launch an investment vehicle that promptly sinks to a 10% or 20% discount from its initial sales price. It tends to discourage investors.

The new closed-ends included a large number of specialized funds, particularly foreign stock funds because stock markets were booming all around the globe in 1986, but in the area of general American stocks it was the year of the hotshot money manager. Martin Zweig, capitalizing on the reputation of his market letter and the publicity of his frequent television appearances, launched the Zweig Fund. He easily raised $300 million, after originally planning to raise a mere $65 million. Mario Gabelli, another "hot hand" money manager, raised $400 million for his Gabelli Fund. Charles Allmon's Growth Stock Outlook Trust rapidly mopped up another $143 million.

You might call this variety of closed-end the One-Man Fund, and it carries with it all the risks of individual human mortality. For what would happen to the fund if the Great Man should be fatally run over by a taxi on his way to Wall Street? To be less melodramatic, what if the Great Man should stumble in his triumphant investment progress? Sooner or later even the greatest stock market genius is going to slip on a banana peel. In the long run, like Napoleon, he may develop hemorrhoids and be unable to concentrate sufficiently on the battle-field at Waterloo. In the closed-end fund business, alas, not even these calamities are necessary.

As an investment adviser before launching his fund, Zweig logged an annual average return of 23.4% after commission expenses from 1980 to 1986. Like the eighteenth-century Duke of Marlborough, who never lost a battle, Zweig never had a year in which followers of his stock-picking service would have lost money. So the Zweig Fund was snapped up at $10 a share in October 1986—and promptly sank to $8.75, at a time when the stock market was breaking new records almost weekly. In early 1987 the Zweig Fund was languishing at 9⅞, and investors with wistful hopefulness were still giving it a 2.8% premium over its asset value at that. Gabelli's and Allmon's funds had already sunk to 4% discounts.

An interesting question is why did these promoters go against the tide to launch a closed-end fund rather than a mutual fund? According to Zweig it was that the closed-end format let him manage the fund without having to worry about shareholders bailing out, as they might easily do if the fund hit a bad patch. The fact is that the Zweig Fund, like many of the new closed-ends, makes it very difficult for shareholders to force a reorganization—to convert it into a mutual fund for example, and so recoup some of their money if the closed-end fund should sink to a deep discount.

This kind of arrangement is "like locking the fire exits at a movie theater," in Herzfeld's opinion, and may lead to even bigger discounts if such a closed-end fund falls into disfavor with investors.

Specialty Funds

The specialty funds divide up into various groups. The biggest, which is listed in a separate weekly table that we will get to further on, is the bond fund group. There are also funds that specialize in convertible bonds; in gold mining companies and precious metals; in one particular industry such as utilities or the oil industry; or in the companies of a particular country, such as Germany, or a specific region, such as Scandinavia.

There are also venture capital funds, which invest in companies that are just starting up, and so offer great hopes of growth—together with equally big risks.

And you also have dual-purpose funds, which issue two kinds of shares, one of which gets all the capital gains while the other gets all the income.

A few funds have their money concentrated to such an extent in only one or two companies that they barely qualify for consideration as closed-end funds. Sterling Capital Corporation, for example, traded on the American Stock Exchange, had about two-fifths of its assets tied up in First Executive Corp. stock in early 1987. And then there are oddballs like Central Fund of Canada, which at the time of writing consists mostly of a large heap of gold and silver bullion and might be a good substitute for buying precious metals when the fund is trading at a discount.

Let us take a quick look at each of these groups.

One-Industry Funds

The number one rule here is: don't buy these funds when they are first issued. The only time their promoters can successfully launch such funds is when the particular industry involved is in the limelight and the public is eager to pay inflated prices for the shares of companies in this currently fashionable area of the stock market. So they are not a bargain to begin with. It also takes time to get the fund organized, approved, and onto the market. By this time the magic may already be beginning to fade, and the biotechnology or medical care stocks or whatever the latest fad is may be ready for a fall.

145

Besides this, you will be paying the underwriter a big, fat commission of about 7%. You might as well buy a load mutual fund in those circumstances.

Specialized funds currently available include newcomers such as First Financial Fund, Emerging Medical Technology Fund, and Pilgrim Regional Bank Shares. Old-timers include Petroleum & Resources Corp. and Japan Fund.

Established funds that concentrate on gold, silver, and precious metal producers include ASA Ltd. (which invests exclusively in South African shares) and Central Fund of Canada (which invests mostly in gold and silver bullion). Another major company in this area is Anglo American Gold Investment Company, but unfortunately its discount or premium from net asset value is not readily available.

Venture Capital Funds

These are rather a raffish crew in a staid and sober industry; they are the most speculative of all the closed-end funds. They put their money into new, unfledged companies that may have great promise but also face a highly uncertain future in a world of giant established corporation competitors. It may be difficult to sell large blocks of these new, untried companies, and so your fund may find itself locked into its investments for better or for worse, for richer or for poorer, for a very long time.

Nevertheless, if you are thinking of taking a flier on a newly formed company that has a patent on hydrogen-powered engines, liquid-display terminals, or security-patrol robots, consider a venture capital fund instead. It will spread your money over perhaps twenty or thirty technically innovative companies, and the chances are that two or three of them will survive and do outstandingly well. And besides, if you follow the advice given in this book, you will buy them all at a discount.

Among this group, which includes some regional funds with a bias toward the Sunbelt, are Capital Southwest Corp., Growth Fund of Florida, and Rockies Fund. As a warning to the less venturesome, Midland Capital Corp. was in bankruptcy proceedings as this was written.

Dual-Purpose Funds

These funds are something like Siamese twins: two funds in one. They have two classes of stock: capital shares and preferred shares. The capital shares get all the capital gains the fund may achieve, and the preferred shares get all the income it produces. A neat arrangement whereby you can double your capital gains potential if that is what you want, or double your income potential if current yield is your main concern. In both cases you get leverage of two to one, which is something like getting a 50% margin loan and not having to pay any interest on it.

In simplified terms it works like this: if the fund starts out with a portfolio worth $10 million, the investors in the capital shares, who put up only $5 million of the total, nevertheless are entitled to the capital gains on the entire $10 million portfolio.

If the dual-purpose fund should subsequently sink to a discount, as it usually does, the leverage for both classes of investor becomes even greater.

When the dual-purpose fund is formed, a specific date is established, usually ten or fifteen years in the future, when the preferred shares will be redeemed at a predetermined price. The owners of the capital shares must then decide whether to liquidate the fund and take their money or convert it into a mutual fund.

This peculiar double-jointed structure leads to price quotations that can easily mislead the unwary investor. The dual fund's capital shares, for instance, might be trading at a huge discount and look like an amazing bargain. But it would only be a bargain if the fund were liquidated today, which it isn't going to be. If you figure in the fact that the preestablished liquidation date is still ten or fifteen years in the future, the big discount merely reflects the unfortunate circumstance that the owner of the capital shares is not going to collect any income from them for ten or fifteen years. So the discounted price simply compensates him for the lost income.

A number of these funds came on the market in 1967, but they have now outrun their allotted span, and there are currently only three available: Global Growth, Gemini II Fund, and ML Convertible Securities.

The dual-purpose fund looks like a great idea at first sight, but on closer inspection it doesn't really work out all that well. The fund management tends to be torn apart by a Jekyll-and-Hyde mentality—should it invest in stocks that provide generous income, or should it concentrate on growth companies to keep the capital shareholders happy? As a matter of practical politics the managers have to steer the middle course into an unhappy compromise.

The dual-purpose funds "are a fine but sad example of jacks-of-all-trades who are masters of none," says Herzfeld. "As their records affirm, they do not meet either of their objectives very well."

You can probably get better results yourself by selecting a fund that concentrates on growth stocks and buying it on margin. Or doing the same with a bond fund if you want income.

Foreign Country Funds

There is a fairly large and growing group of funds that specializes in the company shares of one particular country or region. These include First Australia Fund, First Australia Prime Income, Japan Fund, Korea Fund,

Mexico Fund, France Fund, Germany Fund, Italy Fund, Scandinavia Fund, and the South African fund ASA Ltd.

The current premium or discount on all the above may be checked in the weekly table of quotations in the financial press. Two other funds worth mentioning are Israel Development Corporation and Anglo American Gold Investment Co., which has a huge portfolio of South African shares. But unfortunately these two are not in the weekly table and their discount or premium is not readily available.

Foreign country funds provide an excellent way of building up a worldwide portfolio of stocks at a discount. It is like buying the entire world at 20% or 30% off. If you owned half a dozen of them you might have a much more stable overall investment than if you owned U.S. investments exclusively. The reason for this is that the stock markets of the world are seldom in sync with each other. When American stocks are plunging in New York, Japanese stocks may be soaring in Tokyo. When the Mexico City stock market sinks to a new low, the Paris stock market may be climbing to new highs. By spreading your investments around in various countries, you even out the ups and downs of the U.S. stock market plus the foreign markets balance out each other's fluctuations as well. Global investing is a tricky proposition, however. Even when the closed-end funds do the nitty-gritty work for you of selecting the most promising foreign companies, you still have to juggle three separate variables. First, are you getting your foreign fund at a discount from its net asset value?

Second, how is the American dollar doing against the foreign currency involved? If the dollar is strong against the French franc, for example, that would be a good time to buy the France Fund, because if the greenback should subsequently decline against the franc in foreign exchange dealings, you would profit merely on the difference in the exchange rate. Currency fluctuations can be considerable: the German mark has ranged from less than two to more than four marks per dollar in the last few decades.

Third, how is the foreign stock market doing? Are you buying First Australia Fund just at the time the Sydney stock market is hitting an all-time high?

The rules therefore are these: look for a foreign country fund selling at a discount; buy it if the dollar is strong against the currency of the country involved and if the country's stock market is in a slump. All three things do in fact tend to go together, and they are fairly easy to check in the financial press. Many newspapers run the Associated Press table of daily exchange rates, which lists not only the current rate for more than forty foreign currencies, but also a daily average that shows how the dollar is doing against a basket of ten major currencies. *The Investor's Daily,* which is challenging the *Wall Street Journal* as the nation's main purveyor of solid financial information, runs daily graphs plotting the performance of twelve major world stock markets over the past fifty-two weeks. The *New York Times* and other major dailies run tables with the latest stock index figures of markets from Frankfurt to Sydney. These indexes are the local equivalents of the Dow Jones average or the New York Stock Exchange index in the United States. A particularly elaborate and useful table of foreign stock market indexes is prepared by Morgan Stanley Capital International Perspective of Geneva, Switzerland. The major utility of this table is that it translates the performance of each foreign market from the local currency into U.S. dollars so that you have a uniform basis of comparison. You will find this table in *Barron's* magazine in a weekly column titled "The International Trader."

You may have wondered why Korea Fund was selling at such a big premium and ASA Ltd. at such a huge discount in the table. This brings us to perhaps the most important consideration of all when investing abroad:

international politics. The Korean stock market has been so tightly closed against foreign investors that into the last half of the 1980s Korea Fund was practically the only way for an American to invest in Korea. Investors, meanwhile, were falling all over themselves trying to invest in a country they thought might turn out to be another industrial giant like Japan. That 29% premium, however (which incidentally had risen to more than 70% at times in 1986), was in for a nasty jolt as soon as alternative Korean investments became available to foreigners. In 1987 other Korean funds were available in London and elsewhere. And a few threatening moves by a huge, well-armed communist North Korean army poised just twenty-five miles from the Seoul Stock Exchange would suffice to knock Korean stock prices for a loop, as well as turning that hefty premium into a sizable discount.

In the case of ASA Ltd., the discount reflected the fact that blood was already running in the black townships of South Africa—riots in black neighborhoods, demonstrators killed, the government in a state of siege, foreign countries applying sanctions against South Africa to protest its apartheid racial policy. However, as Lord Rothschild once observed, the time to invest is precisely when the blood is running in the streets. In this case you are investing at a huge discount. A lot of the bad news is already out. Most interesting of all, among U.S. government sanctions is a proposal to ban the purchase of South African securities by American citizens. The application of such a measure might force ASA Ltd. to go into liquidation, and investors might then get full net asset value for the shares they bought at a discount of more than 50%.

In any event, let these two funds serve as warnings that there is usually more than meets the eye of a person who doesn't usually read the foreign-datelined items in his newspaper.

Convertible Bond Funds

There are only three of these funds and they are all pretty much alike in size, the general quality of their portfolios, and their performance: American Capital Convertible, Bancroft Convertible, and Castle Convertible.

They specialize in corporate bonds that can be converted into the company's common stock under certain specified conditions and at a predetermined price. A convertible bond is a useful little hybrid that offers you the twin advantages of the good guaranteed current yield of a bond plus the chance for capital gains if the common stock goes up in price. Evaluating such a bond, however, is rather a complicated matter. Its value depends on such factors as its maturity date, its quality rating, the price at which it may be converted into common stock, and whether it is selling at a price above or below its conversion value.

These are the things you are unlikely to have the time or the expertise to evaluate yourself properly. A convertible bond fund offers you the advantage of a professional management doing all the evaluating for you.

As all three funds are so similar, opt for the one with the biggest discount, and sell the one with the narrowest discount or the largest premium.

Closed-End Bond Funds

There are more than two dozen closed-end bond funds. The crucial information on their current net asset value is contained in a table distributed to the press by Lipper Analytical Services, Inc. You will find this weekly list in *Barron's* magazine, in Wednesday's editions of the *Wall Street Journal* and the *New York Times,* and in other periodicals.

The sample below shows the unaudited net asset value of each fund as of Friday, January 9, 1987. The stock

	N.A. Value	Stock Price	% Diff.
AmCapBd	b22.39	24⅞	+11.1
AMEV Secs	11.31	12¼	+ 8.3
BunkerHill	18.29	22⅞	+25.1
CircleInc	12.94	14⅝	+13.0
CNAInc	b12.04	13¼	+10.0
Currenti	13.46	12¾	− 5.3
DrexelBd	20.89	23⅝	+13.1
Excelsior	18.55	18¾	+ 1.1
FstAustrPr	8.28	8½	+ 2.7
FtDearInc	16.24	16	− 1.5
GloblYldFd	9.66	9⅛	− 5.5
Hatteras	18.12	20⅞	+15.2
INAInvS	19.85	19⅝	− 1.1
IndSqls	18.00	17¾	− 1.4
Intercap	20.95	24⅜	+16.4
JHanInv	23.05	25½	+10.6
JHanSec	17.06	17⅝	+ 3.3
KinwtBAus	9.58	10⅞	+13.5
LinclnNatl	27.46	26⅞	− 2.1
LinclnNatCv	14.59	15¼	+ 4.5
MFSMuniInc	9.47	10⅜	+ 9.6
MMIncInv	11.18	13	+16.3
MntgSt	20.10	22¾	+13.2
MuOmahI	14.18	17¼	+21.7
PacAmInc	b16.46	17	+ 3.3
StateMSec	11.79	13¼	+12.4
TransamI	24.00	25⅞	+ 7.8
USLIFE	10.28	11¾	+14.3
VestFd	14.77	14⅜	− 2.7

price listed is the dealer-to-dealer asked price for the funds quoted over the counter, and the closing market price for the funds quoted on the New York Stock Exchange or the American Stock Exchange.

You may well ask yourself why most of these closed-end bond funds were trading at a premium on January 9, 1987. And more particularly, why a few were selling at a premium of as much as 25% above the fund's net asset value. The answer may be an object lesson on why not to buy closed-end funds at a premium. The main reason here appears to be that investors who in the previous few years grew accustomed to getting double-digit yields from money market funds when interest rates were soaring found that in 1986 and 1987 they were down to a measly 6% or so as interest rates came down.

Looking around for a more lucrative alternative, they switched their money into bond funds (either of the open-end or closed-end variety) where they noted they could still get double-digit yields. Billions of dollars were thus poured out of money market funds into bond funds by investors who did not realize that they were thereby putting their money at a considerably higher risk of loss.

The money market fund is much less risky because it has its capital invested in short-term loans, typically with an average maturity of only sixty, thirty, or even seven days. In such a short time span there is not time for inflation to erode the value of those dollars. And if interest rates go up, the fund can reinvest its money at higher rates almost immediately. The risk of capital loss is thus minimal, so much so that most money market funds give their shares a constant value of $1 which never varies.

However, once you jump out of a money market fund into a bond fund, which has its money invested, say, in thirty-year bonds, you can quite easily lose half your capital if interest rates should rise sharply. The long-term $1,000 bond with a 5% coupon that yields $50 a year will sink in value to about $500 when interest rates rise to 10% and it has to compete with new $1,000 bonds offering a 10% coupon.

When you face this kind of risk, which in the light of experience in recent years seems a fairly large one; when in addition you have the likelihood of thirty years of inflation ahead of you; when, furthermore, interest

154

rates are low and thus more likely to rise than to fall—this is no time to be buying a closed-end bond fund at a premium.

Nevertheless, that is not what the crowd thought. In 1977, when interest rates were high, the average discount on closed-end bond funds was about 5%. In 1978, when they were higher, it widened to 8%.

After the price discount, the next thing to check out in a bond fund is the average maturity of its portfolio. As we have seen, the rule here is: the shorter the better. A fund holding thirty-year bonds faces the threat of thirty years of inflation. Its price will drop much more severely when inflation and interest rates go up than a fund with an average portfolio maturity of only five years. The shorter the fund portfolio's average maturity, the more stable its price will be. The problem is that the average maturity is not a readily available figure; you may have to write for the fund's latest report to stockholders and seek the information there.

To return to a familiar and well-worn point, the next important thing to check is the fund's expense ratio as stated in its reports to shareholders. Herzfeld notes that the average closed-end bond fund has expenses amounting to about 9% of its income, so "if a fund's expense cost is 9% or higher it cannot be truly considered a sound buy unless it is selling at a discount of at least 9% to compensate."

At the time of writing, bond funds with lower expense ratios include John Hancock Income Securities, Montgomery Street, and American Capital Bond Fund.

One further detail to watch is who is running the fund—a bank, a mutual fund management advisory company, or a brokerage house? Funds run by brokerage houses, for reasons that may not be above suspicion, tend to have higher portfolio turnover rates, and actively traded funds tend to have poor-to-mediocre track records.

For closed-end bond funds the central fact of their

existence is interest rates, and a rise in these rates hits them with a double-whammy, because when interest rates go up the stock market generally comes down. So the closed-end bond fund finds that the bonds in its portfolio are dropping in price, and at the same time its own share price is falling because of the gloomy mood in the stock market. And of course this double effect works with equal force in reverse: falling interest rates mean higher bond prices and thus a higher net asset value for the fund, while the fund's share price is boosted by the general stock market euphoria.

Closed-end bond funds also have advantages over buying individual bonds. You buy a diversified portfolio of thirty to sixty bonds in one package instead of one bond—and at a discount too. The discount in turn means a higher yield. And in addition most bond funds pay dividends quarterly or even monthly. Bonds pay only semiannually. The disadvantages are the costs involved: the fund's management fee and operating expenses. There is also the uncertainty about the discount, which may well widen after you buy the fund. Hence, the importance of buying only when the discount is unusually large.

The normal discount may vary from one fund to another for reasons peculiar to each fund, such as the quality of the bonds it holds, the competence of its management, or the average maturity of its portfolio.

"The ideal way to trade bond funds," Herzfeld says, "is to start by buying a fund which not only has the highest discount rate relative to its normal one, but the highest discount relative to what the rest of the group is doing." Provided the bonds in its portfolio are not of exceptionally poor quality or lengthy maturity, we might add.

As with all fixed-interest investments, high inflation (and its usual concomitant of high interest rates) is murderous for closed-end bond funds. At such times, says Herzfeld, "it is essential to hedge long bond fund positions with either short positions in overpriced bond funds or short positions in Treasury bond futures."

Dividend Reinvestment Plans

Just as with any other stock that offers you the opportunity, you can cut down your transaction costs considerably, and even eliminate stock brokerage commissions entirely, if your closed-end fund has a dividend reinvestment plan. Most of the closed-end bond funds and many of the stock funds have such plans.

If you sign up for the Niagara Share systematic investment service plan, for example, your dividends are reinvested automatically for you without going through a broker. There is a 50-cent fee per transaction, and the brokerage fees are greatly reduced because Niagara combines all shareholders' purchases into one big order. Your share of the brokerage fee typically comes to 1% or less of your purchase. An even more valuable feature is that you can also make additional cash investments in the plan of any amount more than $25 at a time, on the same terms.

However with closed-end funds the clear benefits of dividend reinvestment plans for stockholders in other types of companies are somewhat muddied by the peculiar structure of the closed-end fund. The question is: if the fund is selling at a premium or a discount, is the dividend going to be reinvested at the premium price, at the discounted price, or at the net asset value price? Most funds with such plans provide that the dividend and any additional cash be reinvested at the net asset value price if the fund is selling at a premium, and at the market price—which is to say the discounted price—if the fund is selling at a discount on the reinvestment date. However, this is a murky area, since if a fund issues new shares under its dividend reinvestment plan at below net asset value this dilutes the net asset value of the fund and might be considered unfair to the shareholders who do not reinvest their dividends.

Summing Up

Now that you have looked in detail through the wide range of possibilities offered by the different types of closed-end funds, let us come back to the broad overall picture and stress one major point we have only mentioned in passing so far.

Closed-end funds tend to be less vulnerable to sudden market panics than mutual funds are. The reason lies in the structure of the two different types of fund.

When the Dow Jones average starts to plunge and alarmed investors from Oshkosh to Dubuque get on the phone to sell their shares, the mutual fund may be swamped with a rising tide of redemptions, which it is duty-bound to honor. To raise the cash needed to pay them off the mutual fund then has to sell off shares from its portfolio—precisely at the worst possible time, when prices are plunging. When you have nearly 2,000 mutual funds faced with the same avalanche of sell orders and they all have to dump stock at the same time, the mutual funds themselves can have an enormous downward impact on the market and pile-drive prices even lower. This is even more alarming to their investors, who decide to redeem some more mutual fund shares, and the bear market begins to feed on itself.

The closed-end fund, meanwhile, is under no obligation to humor its more panicky investors and can ride out the storm. As Niagara Shares said in its 1985 annual report, "We continue to believe the closed-end structure is superior to that of the open-end mutual fund. Being free of a net redemption problem permits us to concentrate on long-term investment objectives and to base our decisions on fundamentals with minimum regard for short-term factors."

As an example of the difference between the two types of funds, consider September 11, 1986, a harrowing day in which the Dow Jones Average of 30 Industrials plummeted a sickening eighty-seven points—its biggest one-day loss ever—and trading volume also soared to an all-time record. Mutual fund investors did not exactly panic, but the level of redemptions doubled at some funds. In the week of September 11–15 the leveraged funds were particularly hard hit. Hartwell Leverage Fund was down 11.48% in those five days, Steadman Associates down 11.22%, and 44 Wall Street down 11.05%.

Meanwhile the closed-end funds were relatively unperturbed by comparison. The major effect of the market slide on them was a widening of the premium if they were trading at a premium and a narrowing of the discount for those that were trading at a discount at the time. What this meant was that the closed-end funds' portfolios were declining with the rest of the market but their own share prices were holding up relatively better in the absence of panicky investors with a right to instant redemption. Lehman and Source Capital, for instance, were down about 5% each while the stock market was down about 8%.

Early in this chapter we quoted the words of Benjamin Graham chastising the "inertia and stupidity" of closed-end fund investors, and the above episode would certainly seem to confirm their inertia.

However Graham had no great liking for mutual funds either, because in his judgment they were unlikely to do any better than the market averages. They thus offer hardly any opportunity to beat the market, which obviously must be the aim of the intelligent investor.

In his classic work *The Intelligent Investor,* Graham had this to say: "If you want to put money into investment funds, buy a group of closed-end shares at a discount of, say, 10% to 15% from net asset value, instead of paying a premium of about 9% above asset value for shares of an open-end company. Assuming that the future dividends and changes in asset values continue to be about the same for the two groups, you will thus obtain about one-fifth more for your money from the closed-end shares."

Once again we are down to basics. Beating the market means cutting your investment costs, and the discount on the closed-end fund can be a major cost-cutting tool.

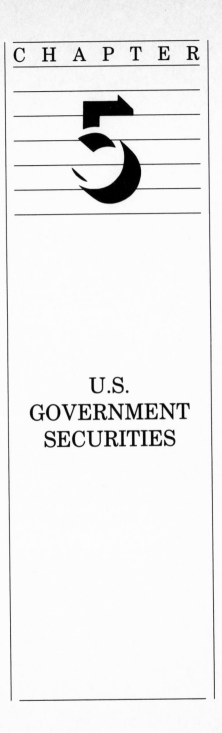

CHAPTER

5

U.S.
GOVERNMENT
SECURITIES

No-Cost/Low-Cost
and Safety Too

As they try to cut their costs of investing and managing their money, many conservative investors don't want to lose sight of another primary consideration in their decisions—safety. It happens that one of the simplest ways to invest at little or no cost is also one of the safest: buying securities issued by the federal government through the U.S. Treasury or through your nearest Federal Reserve Bank or branch. These agencies charge no commissions or fees of any kind. About the only costs they won't cover are your postage or transportation costs to and from the bank or branch and any telephone bills you might ring up in dealing with that bank or branch (check to see whether the office where you do business has a toll-free 800 number).

Though this opportunity may be common knowledge, countless Americans who invest in government securities pay a banker, broker, or mutual fund manager to do the work for them. In some cases they may have excellent reasons for choosing to operate this way. For one thing, they may be unable or unwilling to spend the time necessary to invest directly. For another, they may feel that decisions on such matters as timing and the best maturities to buy are better left to professionals. But let's try to distinguish between authentic prudence or convenience and mere laziness or inertia. If you have the energy to tackle the paper work, why not try buying government securities the no-cost/low-cost way? The government has a new system called Treasury Direct, set up to handle your business, which will be described in detail later in this chapter.

Types of Government Securities

We'll begin by reviewing the three types of securities the government has to offer: (1) savings bonds, (2) Treasury bills, and (3) Treasury bonds and notes.

To many people, the most familiar of these is series EE savings bonds. These well-promoted savings vehicles got their start as a patriotic way to help finance the war effort in World War II. In peacetime they enjoyed continued popularity for many years, until rapid inflation and high interest rates in the late 1970s and early 1980s rendered them just about obsolete. In 1982 the government took the whole program in for a thorough overhaul and modernization and came up with a pretty decent new model. Yet the stigma savings bonds had acquired over the years as stodgy, behind-the-times investments lingered. The next time you are at some social gathering talking sophisticated investments, try bringing up savings bonds. If your experience is anything like ours, you'll be met with silence and blank stares.

All right, there will never be anything flashy or exciting about savings bonds. Still, the idea that they are old hat may itself be old hat. In 1986 the main class of savings bonds, known as series EE, had one of its biggest years ever, selling to the tune of nearly $12 billion. We'll get to the details shortly.

At a more sophisticated level there are Treasury bills, with lives of one year or less; Treasury notes, which generally mature from two to ten years after their issue date; and Treasury bonds, with maturities beyond ten years to a maximum of about thirty years. Bills, bonds, and notes are sold at periodic auctions in which anyone can participate by filling out the appropriate documents and submitting them, along with payment, by specified deadlines.

Beyond their no-cost/low-cost availability, all Treasury securities have several well-known virtues. The most important is the federal guarantee they carry, covering both interest and principal. Behind this guarantee lies an interesting paradox. Suppose you were a profligate spender, living constantly beyond your income and owing more debts than anyone else in the world. You'd expect to have a very poor credit rating, wouldn't you? And indeed you would, unless you were the government of the United States. Budget deficits, mounting national debt and all, the federal government still is regarded today as just about the best credit risk anywhere. It has the power to tax and to print money, sitting atop a huge and (most of the time) vital economy. If there is ever a default on Treasury securities or savings bonds, you can bet that most other types of paper investments will be in dire trouble as well.

Interest on Treasury securities is exempt from state and local taxes—a nice money-saver if you live in a place where such taxes are imposed. Interest on bills, bonds, and notes is subject to federal income tax. However, owners of savings bonds can postpone paying any federal tax until the bonds are cashed in.

How to Buy

Let's suppose you are interested in buying one or more types of Treasury securities but haven't any idea of how to get started. We'll take the simplest type, savings bonds, first. Series EE bonds come in denominations of $50 and up and are sold at a discount from their face value (e.g., a $50 bond costs $25). You can buy them through employers' payroll deduction plans; over the counter at banks, savings and loans, and other financial institutions; or directly from the Treasury or your nearest Federal Reserve Bank or branch. If you are in the market for larger-denomination bonds ($1,000, $5,000, or $10,000), a local bank may not have them in stock. In that case, a bank officer should be eager to forward your order and payment to the Treasury or Federal Reserve.

Not eager at all, you say? He seems harried and irritated at having to deal with this profitless transaction? Well then, at least he can give you a blank order form and you can mail off the order yourself (see the list of addresses at the end of this chapter). Mark the outside of the envelope "ORDER FOR SAVINGS BONDS" or some such, so that the recipients will know where to route it. As for the problem of how to get speedy, cheerful no-cost/low-cost service at the bank, that's a subject for Chapter Six.

Once in hand, the savings bonds should be stowed in a secure place. Our preference is a top-quality safe in one's own home, installed so that it cannot be easily carried away by intruders. If you feel better with a deposit box in a bank vault, so be it. In theory, elaborate security measures aren't necessary. Savings bonds are advertised as "safe and indestructible" by the government, which promises: "If lost, stolen, mutilated or destroyed,

165

the bonds will be replaced without charge upon application—and will bear the original issue dates." Fine, but why expose yourself to the hassle? While you're at it, make a note of the bonds' serial numbers, face amounts, issue dates, and the names in which they are registered, and file that note separately with your other financial records. The information will be handy to have if you ever need to file a request for replacement bonds.

Once you have the bonds socked away, they go to work increasing in value. The progress is admittedly slow at first. An EE bond is not eligible for redemption until six months after you buy it. You must hold it for a full year to get the basic 5.5 percent interest rate. Ideally, you should plan to keep it for at least five years, because at that point the bond qualifies for a more generous "market-based" interest arrangement.

This rate is computed twice a year by the government, at 85% of the average yield available from five-year Treasury securities. Obviously, you're conceding something here—15% of the yield you could get if you invested instead in five-year notes. Wait, though, there's a kicker. Since the savings bond rate is recomputed every six months, it will go up if inflation and interest rates in general increase substantially. That's a good little cushion to protect you against the unforeseen, and it isn't available on any other type of conventional government security.

What if the opposite happens, and interest rates fall to very low levels? In that case, you're protected by a floor. Series EE bonds now being sold are guaranteed to pay at least 6% annually as long as they are held for at least five years. For bonds sold until November 1, 1986, the minimum rate is 7.5% a year, which became very attractive as market interest rates fell in the mid-1980s. So attractive that even Henry Kaufman, the famous Salomon Brothers Inc. economist whose staff tracks every obscure corner of the credit markets, was recommending EE bonds. More attractive, in fact, than the redesigners of the savings bond program ever intended back in 1982. That's why they lowered the floor rate for bonds being sold today. To their credit, they gave the public several months' notice that they were considering the change before they actually made it.

EE bonds are sold with a stated life of ten years. In the past, this maturity has traditionally been extended by the government. Bonds sold in 1941 did not stop earning interest until they were forty years old. However, if interest rates should settle at low levels in the years ahead, the government may not be so eager to extend the life of the highest-paying bonds sold in this decade. Plainly, you do not want any bond that has stopped paying interest sitting around collecting nothing but dust. On the other hand, if you cash it in, you face what authorities on the subject call a "taxable event" of some significance. If you do not need to get at your accumulated interest and principal, there is a way out of this tight spot. You can exchange your EE bonds in any amount of $500 or more for another variety called HH bonds, which pay cash interest at a fixed rate of 7.5% a year. The HH interest is subject to current tax, but you won't have to pay Uncle Sam for what you earned on your EE bonds until the HH bonds are redeemed or mature, ten years after they were issued.

If you are embarrassed to admit that you can't think of anything tonier to do with your money than to put it in savings bonds, tell your friends, "I'm heavily into zero-coupon governments." In truth, there are some important differences between modern zero-coupon bonds, which have been so popular in recent years, and series EE savings bonds. You won't find anybody on Wall Street crouched over a computer terminal trading savings bonds. But the two types of securities are based on the same principle.

Some fanciers of savings bonds have only one major gripe about them. There is a limit of $15,000 purchase price, or $30,000 face amount, on the total quantity of

EE bonds that can be bought in the name of any one person in any single calendar year. If you would like to deal on a grander scale, there is no shortage of other options.

Bills, Bonds, and Notes

With clockwork regularity and on some unscheduled occasions as well, the Treasury holds auctions of debt securities to keep money pumping through the huge machine that is the federal government. Every now and then this occurs in a crisis atmosphere, as when the government has borrowed up to its legal limit and Congress isn't ready simply to rubber-stamp yet another increase in the debt ceiling. Otherwise, however, these auctions are a matter of routine for Wall Street firms that deal in government securities and for many individual investors as well.

Treasury bills in thirteen-week- and twenty-six-week maturities are offered every week, and fifty-two-week bills every month, with a minimum denomination of $10,000 and increments of $5,000 above that point. Bonds and notes, which are sold less frequently, are usually available with a minimum ante of $1,000, except for shorter-term notes, which come in denominations of $5,000 and multiples thereof. Once bills, bonds, and notes have been auctioned, they are traded in a vast "secondary market" that dwarfs the stock market if you use dollar value of trading as a gauge. This secondary market makes Treasury securities a liquid investment, but you should be aware that if you want to buy existing securities or sell before maturity you will need to act through a banker or broker and pay a commission or accept some price concession. The government itself does not handle any secondary-market orders.

A helpful guide, *Buying Treasury Securities at Federal Reserve Banks,* is published by the Federal Reserve

Bank of Richmond (Public Services Department, P.O. Box 27622, Richmond, VA 23261). It used to be available at no charge, but the people at the Richmond Fed told us in early 1987 they planned to start charging $2 a copy with the appearance of the booklet's newest edition (just one of countless examples of why one often has to settle for "low-cost" instead of "no-cost" investing).

For an explanation of how to participate in a Treasury auction, we'll go step by step through a typical case. We're dealing with the government, remember, so there will be some forms to fill out. However, the process isn't much more complicated than opening a bank account or making an initial purchase of mutual fund shares. In fact, with the recent introduction of a system called Treasury Direct, it is very similar. Anyway, people who want to practice the fine art of no-cost/low-cost investing can't be daunted by a little paper work.

The first step is to visit, write, or telephone the agency you want to deal with, such as the Federal Reserve Bank in whose district you live (check the list at the end of this chapter for names and addresses). You'll want to get the form (New Account Request Form PD5182) to open a Treasury Direct account, and tender forms used by auction participants. At the same time, you should ask for details of the procedures followed by the bank or branch in question, and what information services it provides, for instance, perhaps a twenty-four-hour telephone number with recorded messages describing auction results and/or details of forthcoming offerings.

Treasury Direct

In years past, people who bought Treasury securities submitted tenders for them, along with payment, and subsequently received by mail engraved certificates and government checks for any payment due them. Since the late 1970s, the Treasury has been moving to substitute a computerized "book entry" system for the certificates, which can be cumbersome and expensive to deal with. The transition has been accompanied by some controversy and complaints, because a good many investors distrust computers and feel most comfortable with certificates locked away in a safe or safe deposit box. But it has proceeded nonetheless, with promises from the government of "improved services to Treasury securities investors." If all goes according to schedule, by the time you read this, Treasury Direct should be in full effect for all new offerings of bills, bonds, and notes.

Under Treasury Direct, your dealings with the government in Treasury Securities are consolidated in a single account, for which a statement is supposed to be issued each time your holdings change. The account is automatically linked to an account you have designated at a commercial bank or some other financial institution. When any payment is due you, the amount is transferred electronically to that specified account. No check will be mailed to you.

You can, if you choose, submit instructions to open a Treasury Direct account at the same time you submit a tender for your first purchase of government securities. But for simplicity's sake, let's assume you already have an account set up when you are ready to invest.

You have, let's say, $10,000 from a maturing bank certificate of deposit, and decide that when the money comes due you'd prefer to move it into a twenty-six-week (about six months) Treasury bill. From a newspaper or from the Fed's telephone information service, you learn the details of next Monday's bill auction and determine that you want to submit a tender. If you have at hand a standard tender form, you simply fill it out, enclose payment, and submit it to your Fed bank or branch by 1 P.M. on the day of the auction. Instead of the form, you can submit a bid by letter, including the following information:

1. Name or names in which you want the securities to be registered
2. Your mailing address
3. Your Social Security number
4. Telephone number where you can be reached during business hours
5. Face amount of securities you want to buy
6. Type and maturity of securities (in this case, twenty-six-week bills)
7. Your Treasury Direct account number
8. The name, account number, and type (e.g., checking or savings) of your direct deposit account
9. The name of the financial institution where the direct deposit account is held, along with the institution's nine-digit routing number, which may be found printed in those odd but familiar computer numbers at the bottom of a check or deposit slip for the account. If you are uncertain about the number, you can confirm it with a brief phone call to the institution involved.

If you haven't already done so, you will also need to provide the Treasury with an Internal Revenue Service Form W-9, which meets requirements for reporting of interest payments to the IRS. In addition, you may also want to specify whether the tender you are submitting is "competitive" or "noncompetitive." A noncompetitive bidder agrees simply to accept whatever interest rate is determined by the auction; a competitive bidder, by contrast, takes a role in the actual auction by specifying a certain interest rate.

Says the Federal Reserve Bank of Richmond: "Competitive bidders should be quite skilled in the buying of securities or should have professional advice on how to make a proper bid. Many competitive bidders are money market banks, dealers and other institutional investors who buy large quantities of Treasury securities. The yields that these bidders submit for securities depend both on the rates yielded by outstanding money market instruments and on what (if any) movement they think is occurring in short-term or long-term rates.

"Small bidders or inexperienced investors may be better off in submitting a noncompetitive bid. With the noncompetitive bid, prospective purchasers are not required to state a yield. Instead, they simply indicate the amount of securities they wish to purchase and agree to accept the weighted-average yield established in the auction. This assures that their bids will be accepted within certain limitations."

In other words, noncompetitive bidders avoid two risks: first, that they may bid for too low a yield and wind up getting a smaller return than some other participants in the auction; and second, that they might bid for too high a yield, which could mean that their tenders are rejected and their money is returned without having been invested.

The auction itself works this way: the staff of the Treasury Department calculates the average, weighted by size, of all the competitive bids received. This number becomes the yield that all *non*competitive bidders will get. Next, all noncompetitive bids are filled. Then the remainder of the offering is allocated to competitive bidders, starting with the bids calling for the lowest yields and working upward. When the point is reached when all the securities to be auctioned have been allocated to buyers, the highest bid accepted is reported as the "stop-out yield." Bids above that point are rejected.

To consider whether you might want sometime to become a competitive bidder in future auctions, study the results of a given auction and figure out how much more your money might have earned if you were able to get the stop-out yield instead of the average yield. Keep in mind that you must be quite shrewd or lucky to hit the stop-out yield on the nose. The difference between the two yields may be very important to a government securities dealer, working with huge amounts of capital and battling to squeeze a few extra basis points (hundredths of a percentage point) out of an auction. These calculations may well determine whether the dealer sells the securities it buys in the open market right after the auction at a profit or loss. For most individual investors, such concerns don't apply.

The Pros and Cons of Direct Investing

For a moment now, we're going to assume that after reading the past few pages, some readers might be feeling a little grumpy. All those forms—PD5182, W-9, and the rest—who needs them? Why not let a local bank handle all this paper-shuffling? That's their specialty. In this particular type of investing, we'll readily concede that a no-cost/low-cost approach is not for everyone's taste. But we would argue that for lots of people it is well worth the trouble. For one thing, most of the toil comes when you are just starting out. If Treasury Direct lives up to its ambitions, it stands to make a regular program of investing in government securities quite simple.

For another thing, there is the question of after-cost yield. At the time this book was written, a $10,000 investment in a twenty-six-week Treasury bill would earn you about $275. Paying a $40 or $50 fee to someone for handling your transactions would make a serious dent in the return you realize. Minimizing expenses to maximize returns is what no-cost/low-cost investing is all about.

Let's also look at the purposes of choosing to invest in government securities rather than the many alternatives open to any of us. Presumably, buyers of Treasury bills, bonds, and notes want as much safety as they can possibly get. If they buy, say, a ten-year note, they feel absolutely assured of getting a specified amount of

173

interest and their principal back intact a decade hence. "Intact" isn't precisely the right word, of course, since inflation will probably be chipping away at the purchasing power of that principal all through the period when the government has the use of the money. That is true of all investments, however, and the yield available to buyers of government securities at any given time is supposed to contain a built-in "inflation premium" to cover the likelihood of a rise in the cost of living during the security's term.

What if you put your money in an income mutual fund that specializes in government securities? Some of these boast that they can enhance yields to their shareholders with sophisticated trading and hedging strategies and with mortgage-backed securities. But most of these strategies introduce new risks into the equation, and the purpose was to avoid risk as much as possible. Also, these funds, like most mutual funds, represent a continuously managed portfolio that has no single maturity date. In theory, the fund has a perpetual life. That means that the value of the principal ten years from now is unknown. It could be a good deal more, or a good deal less, than $10,000. That, we think, makes a case for giving serious consideration to investing directly in government securities.

Directory for Investors in Government Securities*

TREASURY DEPARTMENT

General Information:
Bureau of the Public Debt
Securities Transactions Branch

*Source: Federal Reserve Board.

Main Treasury Building
Room 2134
Washington, DC 20226
Transactions and account information:
Bureau of the Public Debt, Book-Entry
Washington, DC 20226

FEDERAL RESERVE SYSTEM

Federal Reserve Bank of Boston
600 Atlantic Avenue
Boston, MA 02106

Federal Reserve Bank of New York
33 Liberty Street
(Federal Reserve P.O. Station)**
New York, NY 10045
Buffalo Branch:
160 Delaware Avenue
Buffalo, NY 14202
(P.O. Box 961
(Buffalo, NY 14240)

Federal Reserve Bank of Philadelphia
10 Independence Mall
Philadelphia, PA 19106
(P.O. Box 66
(Philadelphia, PA 19105)

Federal Reserve Bank of Cleveland
1455 East Sixth Street
(P.O. Box 6387)
Cleveland, OH 44101
Cincinnati Branch:
150 East Fourth Street
(P.O. Box 999)
Cincinnati, OH 45201

**Mailing addresses are in parentheses.

Pittsburgh Branch:
717 Grant Street
(P.O. Box 867)
Pittsburgh, PA 15230

Federal Reserve Bank of Richmond
701 East Bird Street
Richmond, VA 23219
(P.O. Box 27622
(Richmond, VA 23261)
Baltimore Branch:
502 South Sharp Street
Baltimore, MD 21201
(P.O. Box 1378
(Baltimore, MD 21203)
Charlotte Branch:
401 South Tryon Street
(P.O. Box 30248)
Charlotte, NC 28230

Federal Reserve Bank of Atlanta
104 Marietta Street, N.W.
Atlanta, GA 30303
(P.O. Box 1731
(Atlanta, GA 30301-1731)
Birmingham Branch:
1801 Fifth Avenue, North
Birmingham, AL 35202
(P.O. Box C-10447
(Birmingham, AL 35283)
Jacksonville Branch:
515 Julia Street
Jacksonville, FL 32231
Miami Branch:
9100 Northwest 36th Street
Miami, FL 33178
(P.O. Box 520847
(Miami, FL 33152)

Nashville Branch:
301 Eighth Avenue, North
Nashville, TN 37203
New Orleans Branch:
525 St. Charles Avenue
(P.O. Box 61630)
New Orleans, LA 70161

Federal Reserve Bank of Chicago
230 South La Salle Street
(P.O. Box 834)
Chicago,IL 60690
Detroit Branch:
160 Fort Street, West
(P.O. Box 1059)
Detroit, MI 48231

Federal Reserve Bank of St. Louis
411 Locust Street
St. Louis, MO 63102
(P.O. Box 442
(St. Louis, MO 63166)
Little Rock Branch:
325 West Capitol Avenue
(P.O. Box 1261)
Little Rock, AR 72203
Louisville Branch:
410 South Fifth Street
Louisville, KY 40201
(P.O. Box 32710
(Louisville, KY 40232)
Memphis Branch:
200 North Main Street
Memphis, TN 38103
(P.O. Box 407
(Memphis, TN 38101)

Federal Reserve Bank of Minneapolis
250 Marquette Avenue
Minneapolis, MN 55480
Helena Branch:
400 North Park Avenue
Helena, MT 59601

Federal Reserve Bank of Kansas City
925 Grand Avenue
Kansas City, MO 64198
Denver Branch:
1020 16th Street
Denver, CO 80202
(Terminal Annex-P.O. Box 5228
(Denver, CO 80217)
Oklahoma City Branch:
226 Dean A. McGee Avenue
(P.O. Box 25129)
Oklahoma City, OK 73125
Omaha Branch:
1701 Dodge Street
(P.O. Box 3958)
Omaha, NB 68102

Federal Reserve Bank of Dallas
400 South Akard Street
(Station K)
Dallas, TX 75222
El Paso Branch:
301 East Main Street
(P.O. Box 100)
El Paso, TX 79999
Houston Branch:
1701 San Jacinto Street
Houston, TX 77002
(P.O. Box 2578
(Houston, TX 77252)

San Antonio Branch:
126 East Nueva Street
San Antonio, TX 78204
(P.O. Box 1471
(San Antonio, TX 78295)

Federal Reserve Bank of San Francisco
101 Market Street
San Francisco, CA 94105
(P.O. Box 7702
(San Francisco, CA 94120)
Los Angeles Branch:
409 West Olympic Boulevard
Los Angeles, CA 90015
(Terminal Annex—P.O. Box 2077
(Los Angeles, CA 90051)
Portland Branch:
915 S.W. Stark Street
Portland, OR 97205
(P.O. Box 3436
(Portland, OR 97208)
Salt Lake City Branch:
120 South State Street
Salt Lake City, UT 84111
(P.O. Box 30780
(Salt Lake City, UT 84125)
Seattle Branch:
1015 Second Avenue
Seattle, WA 98104
(P.O. Box 3567
(Seattle, WA 98124)

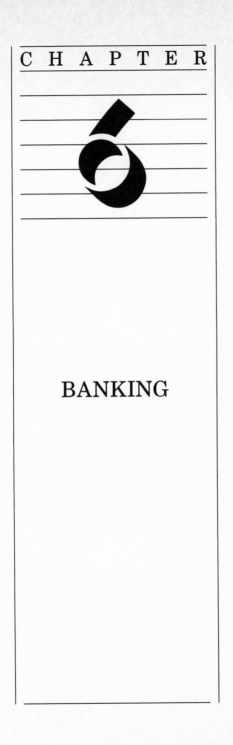

CHAPTER

6

BANKING

Account of an
Errant Account

A couple of years ago a fellow of our acquaintance opened
a money market savings account at a bank in that tem-
ple of finance, New York City. He made his first deposit
with money that had been sitting in an old-fashioned
savings passbook, earning a very low return. In truth,
he had been pretty slow to adapt in the changing world
of savings and money management. Money market investments had been yielding more than passbook accounts for most of the previous ten years. Nevertheless,
he was pleased with himself for having at last caught
up with the times.

A few weeks after the transaction was completed,
there arrived in his mail the first statement for the new
account. It read:

Opening Balance	$682.35

Interest Credit	$4.62
Monthly Account Fee	$8.00
New Balance	$678.92

Monthly account fee? He recalled no mention of such a thing when he opened the account. But there it was on the page, helping to create a financial innovation: the declining-balance savings plan. With some hasty inquiries the matter was resolved. The account was part of a Keogh self-employed retirement program and was therefore exempt from the monthly fee charged by the bank on money market balances of less than $2,500. Still, our friend had had his first taste of banking, 1980s-style.

This is a place populated not only with monthly maintenance fees and below-minimum-balance fees, but also with instant credit card interest charges, annual credit card fees, per check charges, overdraft charges, automatic teller usage fees, even in some places deposit fees. All these, naturally, are anathema to anyone seeking to follow a no-cost/low-cost strategy. Indeed, they make for a harsh environment for all small savers and investors.

But the old, regulated world of consumer banking was no stroll down Easy Street either. Because of limits set by the government on savings account interest rates, banks and savings institutions offered their smaller depositors no access to money market returns. No interest payments at all were permitted on checking account balances. Many states had usury laws limiting the interest rates banks and other lenders could charge on home mortgages and other loans. These had the perverse effect of causing the supply of credit to dry up when the cost of money rose past what lenders could charge. Spells of "tight money" had a nasty propensity for causing or aggravating recessions in housing and other important parts of the economy. They also were a boon to the utterly unregulated breed of "financial services providers" known as loan sharks.

Strong forces pushed for a change in the way consumer banking worked. First of all, deregulation was already in the air in Washington. Though the administrations of Presidents Carter and Reagan may have shared few common themes, deregulation has been one. Secondly, banks and savings institutions were faced with challenges from new, unregulated competitors, including money market mutual funds and central assets accounts offered by brokerage firms (more about both of those subjects later in this chapter). So conditions were ripe for the birth of such wondrous new banking services as money market deposit accounts and checking with interest.

With the opening up of competition, however, banks and savings institutions often had to work harder and pay more to attract deposits. That put pressure on them to cut costs, or, perhaps more expeditious, to pass on to their customers the cost of services those customers formerly might have regarded as "free."

In this section of the book we cannot point you toward any door leading back to the good (or not so good) old days of regulated banking. Nor can we offer any all-purpose system for avoiding all modern banking fees while still availing yourself of modern banking services. It is apparently some sort of immutable law that large and wealthy customers will always get better treatment from banks than small savers and borrowers. However, we will propose a variety of strategies and options open to you in your quest to be a no-cost/low-cost saver, borrower, and manager of your finances.

First, let's take a minute to consider things from the banks' point of view (to save time and repetition, we'll use the term "banks" from here on to refer to all deposit-taking institutions, including savings and loans and savings banks). A big modern bank may deal in just about every conceivable type of financial transaction, but at heart its primary aim may still be simple—to borrow money from depositors and then lend it out again at a higher interest rate. The difference goes to cover its operating costs and to provide for a profit. If there were no prospect of covering costs and making a profit, nobody would want to start a bank or keep it in business.

For a while in the early 1980s, because of wide swings in interest rates, it was possible for a customer to beat many a bank at its own game. Suppose you had a mortgage on your home from the bank, taken out some years earlier, at 7.5% annual interest. Now the bank was forced to offer long-term certificates of deposit at annual interest rates of 13.5%. You could have then bought a CD in the same amount as the balance due on your mortgage, and effectively assured that the bank would pay you net interest of 6% each year until the CD matured. As delightful as these circumstances might have been, they were also dangerous and they could not have persisted indefinitely without severe consequences. For customers as a group, the answer to dealing successfully with banks is not to drive them out of business.

Cost-Conscious Banking

If we don't want to exterminate them, we nevertheless need to approach banks with care, knowing that while they offer their services as allies, they are also in a very real sense our adversaries. Before opening any account at any bank, it is wise to ask for a detailed description of all costs and fees that may be charged. Suppose we're talking about a simple checking account. How much does a depositor need to keep with the bank to avoid a per check charge or monthly maintenance fee? If the minimum balance required isn't met, what are the specific fees per check and per month?

In the case of an ordinary savings account, how is the interest rate determined? (With the advent of full deregulation, some standard 5.5% passbook accounts quietly became 5% or 4.75% passbook accounts.) What minimum balance is required to earn that interest rate, and what balance is required to earn any interest at all, or to avoid "negative" interest of the type we encountered at the beginning of this chapter?

Asking, asking, asking can of course be a tedious and unpleasant process. It has been our experience that many banks have not yet figured out a way to train and keep employees who have the knowledge, the skill, and the time to handle all the transactions that come to them. Certainly, most bank paper work has not yet caught up with bank deregulation, if it is ever going to. At the risk of being trite, let us say that a good measure of comparison shopping is in order. These days comparison shopping may be done not only among institutions with offices in your community, but on a much broader scale. A lot of bank marketing these days is done by mail, for services ranging from credit cards to CDs to home equity loans. At least one newsletter (*100 Highest Yields*, Box 088888, North Palm Beach, FL 33408-8888, $84 a year for fifty-two issues) tracks national consumer banking trends.

In 1986, for example, *100 Highest Yields* turned up "one checking account you won't want." It was a Super-NOW, or interest-bearing, checking account offered by a large California institution. At the time, the bank offered to pay 5% interest on balances of more than $2,500, 4.9% on balances between $1,000 and $2,500, and 4.75% on balances below $1,000. For balances below $2,500, in addition, the bank charged a monthly fee of $7.50, plus 40 cents for each check written. Below a $1,000 balance, the monthly fee was increased to $10. It doesn't take long with a pocket calculator to determine that this was a poor deal for anyone with less than $2,500 to keep in the account. Even above that point, it didn't look so good when you considered that $2,500, invested in other types of bank accounts available at the time, would have returned more than 5%. So who was the natural customer for this account? No one.

The same year, *100 Highest Yields* reported on a Hartford, Connecticut, institution that told its depositors to raise their balances in money market accounts and CDs to at least $10,000 or face a $100 penalty. To people who met this ultimatum, the institution offered a small increase in yields. But it was still plainly playing an adversarial game.

It's tough to formulate any general rules that might simplify the business of seeking out good banking services at low or no cost. While we might say that looking far and wide broadens your options, the best choice might lie in your own backyard, especially if that backyard is a small town where banking has not yet become "sophisticated." A colleague of ours who moved to New York from a town in Kansas in the 1970s still marvels at the experience he had when he closed out his old savings account. The check came with a letter from the president of the savings and loan in Kansas, thanking him for "this nice account" (it amounted to about $10,000) and wishing him well. To his knowledge, our colleague says, he never had met this fellow, but he remembers him fondly and has not yet met his likes in the Greater New York Metropolitan Area.

Furthermore, taking a broad-scale approach may go against one of the best tactics available to you to cut your banking costs. This is simply to find a single good bank and do all your banking there. Such an approach is sometimes spoken of as "relationship banking," and many institutions have some obvious reasons for liking the idea. In order to woo you into such a relationship, a bank may offer many breaks on costs and interest rates—free checking, preferential loan treatment, and so forth. These enticements give you clear-cut benefits in many cases. But if you are leery of getting too entangled with

187

any given institution, you might set up the relationship with as few long-term commitments (e.g., ten-year certificates of deposit) as possible. After all, this is money we're dealing with, not love.

Banking Beyond Banks

We've talked a great deal in this book about how financial deregulation is supposed to increase competition and allow for greater freedom of choice. Logically, that should mean that banks would be under pressure from other types of institutions offering similar services. In practice a good many traditional banking functions can today be found elsewhere. You can write checks, for example, on an account at a money market mutual fund. Loans at appealing interest rates can be had through a central assets account offered by a brokerage firm.

Before we consider these alternatives in detail, we must stress one point that should never escape anyone's attention: the question of safety. If you are banking at a bank, you want to be covered by federal deposit insurance. As recent cases in Ohio and Maryland have demonstrated, state or private insurance cannot be presumed to be as solid as the guarantee of the federal government. So it stands to reason that if you take your business to some other kind of financial institution, you want to examine closely the insurance it offers. A money market mutual fund, for example, may have an impeccable operating record but carry no form of protection against loss at all, unless it is held in a brokerage account that is backed by the Securities Investor Protection Corp.

One of the most common alternatives to a bank or savings institution is a credit union. To many people, the biggest appeal of credit unions is convenience. However, in the best case a credit union should also take advantage of the special rules under which it operates to offer attractive interest rates to both savers and borrowers, and no-cost/low-cost money management as well. Credit unions are nonprofit cooperatives, owned by their members, and thus do not have to pay the income taxes normally levied on profit-making financial services firms. Competitors grumble a lot about this, but that's not your worry. What you want to see, naturally, is a credit union that turns this situation to your benefit by paying you more or charging you less. What's more, many credit unions are subsidized by employers at places of business or other organizations where they operate. The employer may provide free office space and pay staff salaries. To whom should the benefits of this subsidy flow through? The owners, of course—that is, the people who save and borrow at the credit union.

As their setup suggests, you can't just pick any credit union you fancy, the way you can shop around for a banker or broker. Membership in credit unions is limited to people who share some specified common bond, e.g., the employees of a company or members of a religious or fraternal group. That leaves you, to some extent, at the mercy of chance. The place where you work or worship may offer an efficient, aggressive credit union that provides many valuable services. Or it may have a lackadaisical operation, rent by politics. If you encounter the latter, you are not necessarily powerless to do anything about it. Join, and you become part of the democracy that is supposed to decide how it will operate. In our experience, however, we have heard complaints about corporate credit unions that seem to favor only those members with the title of vice-president and above. We have also seen cases where militant employee groups sought to set agendas for credit unions that had little to do with the financial interests of individual members. For information on credit unions, including where to find one or even how to start one, you can write the Credit Union National Association, P.O. Box 431, Madison, WI 53701.

189

Money Market Funds

Since the 1970s, many Americans have entrusted what they consider their "savings accounts" to money market mutual funds—funds that invest in short-term interest-bearing securities such as Treasury bills, commercial paper issued by corporations and, yes, large certificates of deposit sold by banks. For most of their short history, the prime selling point of money funds has been high yields. At times, they have returned twice, even three times, what you could get from a traditional passbook savings account. If this were all they had going for them, though, they would almost surely have fallen out of favor in the past few years as money market interest rates nose-dived. That hasn't happened.

"Probably the most significant reason for their continued success is the convenience they allow businesses, corporations, and others who would be unlikely to shift to stocks or savings banks," observed the United Mutual Fund Selector, an investment advisory service. "Also, brokers often put their customers', as well as their own, money into these funds as a temporary parking lot. Safety of principal is an important aspect, especially to the small investor."

And just how safe is that principal? Unlike almost all other types of mutual funds, money funds seek to hold their net asset values constant through all the ups and downs of the markets. No money fund is covered by federal deposit insurance, but the industry's operating record is excellent. If even modest risk disturbs your sleep, you can choose a fund that invests solely in U.S. government securities. Of course, we have already discussed how to buy those same securities on your own. Most money funds conform pretty well to the standards of no-cost/low-cost investing. Fund sponsors do collect annual fees from the assets of the funds for management and expenses. The management fee and expense ratio should be low, however, by comparison with a stock or bond fund. Any money fund worth your consideration should impose no charge for buying or redeeming shares or check writing. Though most funds permit checks to be written only in amounts of $500 or more, some set minimums of $250, $100, or even less.

Central Assets Accounts

Using money funds as a foundation, numerous investment firms—discount brokers as well as "full-service" ones—in recent years have established accounts designed to consolidate most or all of your financial activities through a single channel. The idea was pioneered by Merrill Lynch, whose Cash Management Account has attracted more than 1 million customers since its debut in 1977. As they spread, they acquired the generic name "central assets accounts."

In addition to money fund investing, these accounts usually provide for investment brokerage, check writing, and a credit or debit card. With this broad array of services, not surprisingly, you need to be aware of the possibility of an equally broad array of fees and charges. To start with, there is the annual maintenance fee for the account itself, which can run to $50, $75, or higher. The firm involved might also charge you for: use of the credit card, check writing, return of canceled checks, brokerage commissions, interest on margin loans . . . in short, this could quickly become a very expensive "convenience." Furthermore, to open one of these accounts you must usually come up with a specified minimum deposit of $5,000, $10,000, $20,000, or more in cash and/or securities.

A cost-conscious approach to these vehicles makes a lot of sense, because none of the individual items that make up a central assets account is proprietary or unique. Any good firm can offer you a Visa, Mastercard, or American Express card; provide you with checks; handle your stock transactions; and so forth. Here, then, is our suggested battle plan for picking a central assets account:

Start by looking at sample monthly statements, ruling out any that are hard to decipher or seem badly organized. You are buying convenience, remember, and you're not likely to get much of it if the basic means of communication causes you to stumble. Then check for:

- An account with a low annual fee, or one that may be waived altogether if the account balance stands above a specified level
- Discount, rather than full-service, brokerage commissions
- A credit card with no annual fee and low interest rate if you plan to use it to borrow in any significant amount
- No charge for check writing, checks, and return of canceled checks (if you are like us, you still rely heavily on files of canceled checks for your financial records and preparing your tax returns)
- A provision for timely "sweep" of your idle cash into the account's money fund, where it can earn interest while it is not otherwise occupied.

In the real world, it will most likely be hard to find a single account that earns a perfect score on all these points. But you can pick the one that comes the closest, especially in those aspects that matter most to you. While you are conducting your search, don't overlook any versions of central assets accounts that might be offered by banks. If we're looking to brokers to serve some of the purposes that used to be fulfilled by banks, it is only fair turnabout to let banks fight back, if they are able and ready to do so.

A Handle on
Credit Card Costs

After you have picked the best institutions to deal with and the best accounts to maintain there, there is still plenty that can be done to cut the costs of managing money, leaving more of it to do the productive work of increasing your wealth and purchasing power. One prime target that we have only mentioned in passing so far: credit cards. We'll assume here that no lengthy peroration against the evils of the credit card is either necessary or desirable. Credit cards surely get more people in financial trouble than any other type of debt. For those people, often the only sound way to deal with credit cards is to cut them in pieces and throw them away. However, if you can manage them prudently, they can serve at best as a useful convenience. For good or bad, they are part of the financial currency of the modern American economy.

A good way to approach the task of keeping down credit card costs has been suggested by the American Financial Services Association, a trade group of firms that provide loans and other financial services to consumers and small businesses. This may not seem like a strictly impartial source of advice. But who has a greater stake in encouraging people to use credit enthusiastically without going overboard?

"People use credit cards for a variety of reasons," the Association noted in its monthly *Consumer Finance Bulletin*. "So the same kind of card is not always the best option for everyone. Some people simply have a major credit card so that they'll have the necessary identification to cash checks, to make hotel reservations, or to rent cars. Others, estimated at about 40% of the people who hold credit cards, use them as cash substitutes or transaction devices. They find it more convenient to be able to use a card, instead of cash or a check, to buy things that they need. Most of the time these cardholders pay off their credit card bills in full each month. Thus, these 'nonrevolvers' usually don't pay a finance charge, since they don't have an outstanding balance from month to month. The majority of people who hold credit cards use them to purchase items or services. But instead of paying off the full amount each month, they pay only a portion of their balance. Since only a part of the total amount charged is paid, these people are actually borrowing money and they pay a finance charge on their outstanding balance."

It may be that none of these three categories precisely describes how you use credit cards. But it makes sense to consider which one fits the best, because each group has its separate set of priorities to consider in choosing the card that will yield the greatest benefits for the lowest cost.

Pure "identification" users don't have to worry much about the interest rate charged, since they don't use their cards to borrow. What they are most likely to want is a card that is widely recognized, at no or the lowest available annual fee. A "premium" card embossed in some precious-metal color wouldn't have much appeal for them, except possibly for the purported prestige element. We don't think many no-cost/low-cost investors are much swayed by promotional gambits like "one look and you know it's a card of distinction."

The "nonrevolver," who uses a card to buy but not to borrow, also logically wants one with no, or a very small, annual fee. If you are in this class, however, you also should look for something else—a generous "grace period" between the time purchases are made and the date when the clock starts running on interest charges. Grace periods can vary widely even between issuers of the same card. And as some banks have lowered credit card interest rates in the past year or two, they have also shortened or eliminated grace periods. "Also important are other fees, such as a fee for each transaction on the card or late charges or over-limit charges," the American Financial Services Association said. "To many nonrevolvers, the amount of the credit limit is also a factor, especially if the card is used for business travel or other travel and vacation expenses, where charges can accumulate rapidly."

Credit card borrowers, by contrast, need to be concerned with the percentage interest charged, as well as other terms of the credit agreement, including the method used to compute outstanding balances. For heavy users of plastic credit, the annual fee is a relatively small item in the overall equation. We have no desire to take any moral stand on the question of whether you or anyone else should be a "revolving credit user." One of the nice things about money is the privilege of using it according to your own taste and preferences. Still, we do think we are justified in taking a viewpoint toward credit card borrowing on practical, and maybe even esthetic, grounds. Barring some unlikely change in the future, credit card debt remains an expensive and undisciplined way to borrow. That makes it hard to fit sensibly into any consistent no-cost/low-cost strategy for managing money.

Banking on Your Home

The new tax system in this country has exalted the status of homes as a source of credit. While it is phasing out the tax-deductibility of other types of consumer interest, the law provides that interest on most loans secured by a first or second home remains fully deductible. That preserves the cherished write-off for mortgage interest, and it also makes second mortgages, or home equity loans, appealing for many people who own properties that have increased in value over the years. Banks, brokers, and lenders of all sorts have been busy lately pushing home equity loans as a way to finance educational bills, home improvements, even consumer purchases for things like cars or vacations.

All this makes us a little uneasy, and many people we talk to confess to a similar feeling. Call us old-fashioned or not, we tend to balk at the idea of borrowing more than necessary on what for most people and families is their most valued asset. On the other hand, it would be silly to leave a deep well of equity in your home untapped if you need money for something important like college tuition and can't obtain it readily anywhere else. If you are used to dealing with credit successfully, it's hard to argue against taking a deductible home loan over some other nondeductible proposition.

As they bid for your business, whether you are in the market for a mortgage to buy your first home or are seeking a new credit arrangement on a property you already own, lenders emphasize interest rates. That has been especially true in the last couple of years, with mortgage rates having fallen to their lowest levels of this decade. Given the chance, anybody would be eager to trade in an 11% loan for a 9% one. Of course, it's rarely such a simple matter. With home loans of any type, costs are a paramount concern.

Many mortgages offered these days come heavily loaded at the front end with "points," sometimes also called loan origination fees. In a typical situation you might face the choice of a 10¼% fixed-rate loan with one point, or a 9¾% loan with three points. (A point is 1% of the amount to be borrowed, for example, $750 on a $75,000 loan. Three points on that same loan would add up to the considerable sum of $2,250.) How to choose? As a rule of thumb, *100 Highest Yields* suggested, over the full term of a mortgage a point up front raises the cost of the loan by about a quarter of a percentage point. So the two alternatives described above would be roughly equal. If you could pay the points without undue difficulty and expected to be in the house for many years, you ought probably to opt for the 9¾% mortgage with the three points. If, on the other hand, you envisioned owning the house for just a few years before moving on, the 10¼% mortgage with one point would probably make more sense.

Though points are usually the biggest cost item that comes with obtaining a new mortgage, they are by no means the only one. A lender may also charge fees for processing the loan application and for other administrative details. As anybody who has ever bought a house will attest, you need to bring a full checkbook to the meeting at which the purchase is closed. Many or all of those closing costs can arise all over again when you refinance an existing mortgage. Refinancers should also be mindful of the number of points charged on the new loan. The Internal Revenue Service has taken the position that these points cannot be fully deducted in the year in which they are paid, but must be spread out over the life of the loan for tax purposes.

When you are dealing with home equity loans, you are likely to run into some of the same problems, and some entirely different ones as well. Let's suppose you bought a house some years ago for $80,000, and it now could sell for about $200,000. On your original $65,000 mortgage, the balance owed has been paid down to $60,000. Thus you have built up an equity position in the house of $140,000—the current market value minus the money still owed on the mortgage. You could choose to refinance with a new, larger mortgage of, say, $100,000, and thereby pull $40,000 in cash out of your investment. But that course of action might have several drawbacks. For starters, the old mortgage could well carry a fixed interest rate that you still couldn't match on a new loan. Beyond that, you might be at a stage in life where you don't want to commit yourself to a new thirty-year mortgage.

Home equity loan accounts provide an alternative option. Under such a setup a banker, broker, or some other lender would extend you an open credit line of, say, as much as $105,000, or 75% of your equity in the house. You could borrow against that credit line at any time of your choosing, simply by writing a check on the account. Thereafter, you would be responsible for monthly interest payments, but the principal could be repaid as you saw fit. The interest rate on the amount borrowed would "float" according to some prescribed formula, e.g., 1.25 percentage points above the lender's posted "prime" lending rate for its biggest and best customers. Attractive interest rates like this are often available on home equity loans because the collateral is specific, easy to keep track of, and generally considered very solid. This arrangement would let you borrow precisely what you need, and only when you need it, for something like educational tuition bills that might be paid in installments through the school year. It would also let you pay off the loan quickly, with no hassle, should you receive an unexpected bonus or inheritance, or surprise yourself by hitting a home run in the stock market. And it would **also** let you pay the loan off more slowly than you planned if no windfalls should come your way.

Sounds pretty good, you may be saying to yourself. What's the catch? Make that "catches":

1. As soon as you borrow through a home equity loan account, you increase the leverage on your investment, opening yourself up to greater risk as well as greater opportunities. A layoff, a disabling accident, or anything else that interferes with your cash flow might well put you in peril of losing your house if you could not keep up with both the primary mortgage and the home equity loan.
2. A "floating" interest rate can, if events work out that way, float up, up, and away, making a home equity loan a much more expensive proposition than you planned for.
3. A flexible arrangement for repayment of loan principal can bring problems as well as benefits.

It requires a measure of self-discipline on your part to see that the entire amount borrowed doesn't sit unpaid indefinitely. In many home equity loan accounts, the lender has the right to "call" the balance due after a stated interval, such as ten years. When you owe a large debt, ten years can positively fly past.

Then, to get back to the theme of this book, there is the matter of costs to be considered. In order to establish that you really have $140,000 equity in the house, the lender is likely to insist on a professional appraisal of its market value. It also will probably want to collect fees for processing your application and setting up the account. Whether these charges are figured separately or lumped into a single number, the total can come to as much as 2% of the credit line extended (as distinct from whatever amount you might sooner or later actually borrow). That's roughly analogous to two points on a mortgage. Once the account is open, the lender may well charge you an annual maintenance fee whether you borrow any money or not. In fact, the charge may be greater if you don't borrow, since a lender has a hard time making much money from an unused credit line to which it has committed a ready supply of its capital. The agreement may also allow the lender to charge an early close-out fee if the account is closed within a specified period of time, or if it is closed at any time without ever having been used.

In describing the finer points of home equity loan accounts, we've had to talk in generalizations rather than in specific numbers because these accounts are still relatively new, and the marketplace hasn't yet shaped them into any reliable format. It is no rash prediction to say that they are likely to become more and more common and more and more competitive in the next few years. As no-cost/low-cost investors, we'd like to see that competition drive down the fees associated with these accounts. As realists about the modern world of financial services, we'll wait to see such a thing actually happen before we can work up much excitement about it.

However they evolve, it seems clear that home equity loan accounts are best suited for people who have serious purposes in mind for the money they want to borrow, and have a pretty good idea of when and how much. In their present form, that's the way they make the most sense for cost-conscious investors.

A Resolution

Gosh, we've used up just about all the space we allotted for this chapter without getting to some very important questions about banking. Such as, why is it that cards for teller machines, no matter how carefully stowed in our wallets, immediately scratch their delicate surfaces, rendering themselves unusable? Or, whatever happened to toaster giveaways when you open a new account? (Actually, we are delighted to see the appliances gone from the lobby. They were an insult to our intelligence, and represented the worst kind of irrelevant bank marketing.)

But if we haven't got time for all those questions, we will conclude with a firm resolve. We will pay off any and all of our revolving credit balances due, and keep them paid before they incur any future interest charges. We will seek out institutions with reasonable minimum-balance requirements and consistently meet those requirements. We will keep looking for banks where we can have "relationships" without getting bear-hugged to death. Some of these things we will do, even knowing they are just what banks want us to do, since they provide the banks with a handy way to turn some of our money into more or less permanent deposits.

Why? Because the alternative is to pay all those per check, monthly, and annual charges. And we hate spending money just to manage our money.

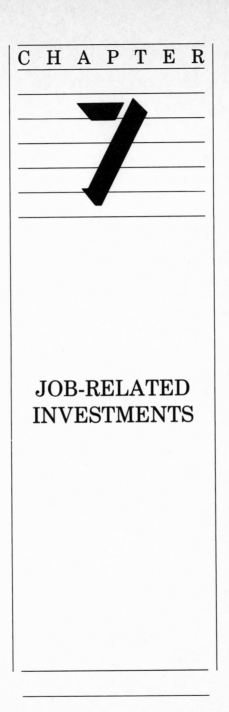

JOB-RELATED INVESTMENTS

Making Real Money
While You Work

Are you a full-time investor or just a part-timer? You may think of yourself as an investor only when you are buying a certificate of deposit at the bank, reading *Barron's* magazine over the weekend and trying to decide on a good mutual fund, scanning the *Wall Street Journal* stock tables on the commuter train to check the latest quote on a likely speculative stock, or reading a book such as this one in the evening for investment ideas.

These are all part-time activities, and only peripheral to your real life: your job and your career.

Remove those mental blinkers. Widen your mental horizons. Your whole life is an investment, and the major part of that investment is your job. So stop and ask yourself: what kind of an investment have I got here?

Is my job a place where I just make a salary to get by on? Or is it a place where I actually make money for myself?

So far in this book we have talked about your own personal savings and investment plans: no-load mutual funds, stocks with dividend reinvestment plans, low-cost banking services. This is really all surplus material, whatever is left over in money, after you have paid your living expenses, and in energy, after you have finished your working day.

But what about the core of your life? Your job, your profession, whatever it is you do to survive? Is this an investment too? Or is it just a means of surviving?

Look at it this way. At some point you will have to stop working, and the core of your life will be gone. What is going to take its place? What are you going to live on then? First, Social Security. Second, whatever you have managed to save and invest. This may not be a very alluring prospect. But there are three other possibilities you may not be paying much attention to, and they are all connected with your job. They are pension plans, profit-sharing plans, and employee stock ownership plans.

Does your job provide these three benefits? If it does you are a full-time investor; if not, a part-timer. And the time to start planning these investments into your future is as early in your working life as you can.

ESOPs: Fables? No; Fabulous? They Can Be

An ESOP (Employee Stock Ownership Plan), like a non-contributory pension plan or a profit-sharing plan, is an investment where the price is exactly right. It costs you nothing. All contributions are made by your employer. If you think your company is a real winner, there is an additional feature in some ESOP plans: you are allowed to chip in some of your own money in addition. But this is strictly up to you.

The basic idea of the ESOP is that the company gives away stock to its employees. Philanthropy? No, not necessarily. The company gets some tax breaks and usually a highly motivated work force.

The government has been pushing the ESOP concept vigorously. Congress, which loves giveaways—particularly if other people give them away—has passed more than a dozen laws promoting ESOPs in the past fifteen years, as a means of broadening the base of capitalist ownership in the American economy and bringing about a more equitable distribution of wealth. More than fifteen states have also passed laws promoting the use of ESOPs.

Largely as a result of this, employee ownership is one of the fastest-growing trends in American business. According to the National Center for Employee Ownership, a nonprofit research organization, by mid-1986 about 7,000 companies with over 10 million workers had employee ownership plans of one kind or another. As recently as 1974, only 300 companies had such plans.

The Center remarks that a growing body of independent research points to two conclusions: companies at least partly owned by their employees "are more financially successful than their competitors, and their employees are accumulating an impressive capital stake."

In its 1986 study "Employee Ownership and Corporate Performance," the Center found that companies improve their performance after setting up ESOP plans. And in a 1984 study partly funded by the New York Stock Exchange, it found that publicly held companies with employee ownership plans outperformed their competitors.

An ESOP is a federally qualified employee benefit program similar to profit-sharing plans in some ways, but with some unique features. Firstly, the ESOP is required by law to be invested primarily in the stock of the sponsoring company. Other employee benefit plans put their money in a number of other investments. The ESOP can also borrow money, and get a tax break in doing so. This could place the employee's benefits at risk, but the ESOP is required to provide employees with contributions equal to the amounts it borrowed.

The ESOP differs from the pension plan in that it does not guarantee a certain benefit at retirement. The pension plan is a defined benefit plan; the ESOP and the profit-sharing plan are not. They are not required to produce a stated, predetermined retirement income for you. They are thus riskier because your company may not be profitable and its stock may go down in price. But in inflationary times a highly profitable company's ESOP could be a gold mine compared to its fixed-income pension plan.

To establish an ESOP a company sets up a trust to hold the assets and makes contributions to it of company stock, or cash to buy stock. The company contributions are tax-deductible up to 25% of the payroll of the participants in the plan. The company can also have the ESOP borrow money to buy more shares of company stock. This is known as a leveraged ESOP.

Usually, all full-time employees with more than one year of service are eligible for the ESOP. Stock is allocated to them in proportion to their pay, in some cases with an increasing allotment as they pile up years of seniority.

If you are a participant in an ESOP, you pay no tax on the stock while it is in the trust. You thus share in your company's capital growth over the years and your tax payments are deferred while your stake is piling up.

Companies like ESOPs for a number of reasons. One is that an ESOP can be used to borrow money cheaply and then repay the loan in pretax dollars. The company gets another tax break when it issues new stock to the ESOP to provide a tax-deductible employee benefit.

And then there are special situations. The founder

or owner of a closely held company wants to retire. He sets up an ESOP and sells the company to his employees. His contributions to the ESOP are tax-deductible.

This might make you wary of some ESOPs. Perhaps the owner is trying to dump an unprofitable company that he is unable to sell in any other way. However, in a September 1985 study of 100 representative ESOP companies, Jonathan Feldman and Corey Rosen of the National Center for Employee Ownership found that "contrary to popular impression, ESOPs are not most commonly used in failing firms—only 1% to 2% of all plans are set up in such cases. More typically ESOPs are used to buy out the retiring owner of a profitable, closely held company, to provide an additional benefit for the employees, or to raise capital through the ESOP ownership technique. Such well-publicized uses as buying a plant that would otherwise close, trading stock for wage concessions, or using an ESOP as part of a leveraged buyout to prevent a hostile takeover, account for less than 3% of all plans."

"The typical ESOP," according to Feldman and Rosen, "owns about 15% to 40% of company stock. Most of the plans are in companies with 100 to 1,000 employees, but they are distributed across all types and sizes of industries."

The study of 100 ESOP companies found that the average company contributed about 10.1% of its payroll to its ESOP from 1980 to 1984, and that taking into account changes in the stock price, "workers at the 1983 median wage level of $18,058 would receive over $31,000 worth of stock after ten years, and more than $120,000 after twenty years from their ESOP plan."

Workers earning $27,000 in 1983 would get about $45,000 after ten years, about $185,000 after twenty years, and about $600,000 after thirty years, the study found.

Feldman and Rosen concluded their study with this

206

question: "Do ESOPs provide a significant source of additional wealth for employees? The data suggests that the answer is yes. Employees who stay with the typical ESOP for more than a few years will begin to accumulate capital that will grow to five or even six figures during their tenure. Just from their ESOP, millions of employees can expect to accumulate financial assets greater than the net financial assets of most American families."

They observed that ESOPs would normally be preferable for younger, more mobile employees, while pension plans would normally be more attractive to older employees or those planning to make a career with a single firm.

"Workers leaving an ESOP plan usually receive a lump sum of money. By reinvesting this money they can see their benefits actually grow, whereas a pension plan will normally shrink in real dollars unless an inflation adjustment feature is included," they said.

But there is nothing like one specific example to drive home the generalities about the money you can make right on the job when your company offers you an ESOP.

One outstanding employee stock ownership plan is that of MCI Communications, a scrappy little company that started out in 1968 with the incredible cheek of taking on the Bell System, the largest private enterprise in the world, as a competitor in long-distance telephone service. By 1979 MCI was serving 180 metropolitan areas at rates 30% to 50% below Bell's, and had 1,200 employees. In April of that year MCI set up an ESOP in which employees automatically participated after one year of service. MCI contributes stock equal to 5% of the pay of covered personnel. MCI, according to some employees (there are now more than 13,000 of them) stands for Money Coming In.

The company's revenues doubled and redoubled and the price of its stock tripled, to the delight of the ESOP participants. Some of MCI's longer-term employees accumulated very substantial stakes in MCI stock. They were helped along in this by the fact that MCI also has an employee stock purchase plan which allows employees with more than three months on the job to devote up to 10% of their paychecks to the purchase of MCI stock, which they get at a 15% discount. Annual MCI stockholder meetings in recent years have been huge, packed with employee-owners interested in the future of the company.

Nevertheless, the sun does not shine forever on even the best and most generous of companies, a point to remember when a large part of your financial future is tied up in an ESOP. For MCI the stormy weather arrived in the 1980s with the wholesale deregulation of the telephone business. Competition, price cuts, and rising costs slashed the company's profits and forced it to lay off 15% of its 16,000 workers in 1986. Union organizers picketed MCI installations and filed forty unfair labor policy complaints. It is at such times that you realize your need for other investments less tied to your employer's fortunes than an ESOP, no matter how fabulous that ESOP seemed at first sight.

However, an ESOP is still something you should keep firmly in mind when looking for a job. The National Center for Employee Ownership, 927 South Walter Reed Drive, Suite 1, Arlington, VA 22204, has a regularly updated, annotated list of 260 companies in which the majority of the stock is owned by employees, and a second list of 230 companies in which employees own a minority of the stock. Try your public library first. The lists are expensive at $100 each.

For $10 you can get a directory of ESOP companies from the ESOP Association, 1725 DeSales Street, N.W., Suite 401, Washington, DC 20036. The Association is a nonprofit organization of companies with ESOP plans, and its list of members covers almost every size and type of company in every region of the United States.

Profit Sharing:
All Pure Profit for You

If the company you are working for does not have a profit-sharing plan, start looking around for a job in a company that does. It is not only that you will be better off yourself; research has shown that companies with profit-sharing plans consistently outperform those that don't. They are not only more generous companies; they are also better, more competitive companies, where you can feel more secure about still having a job thirty years from now.

Such companies are really not too hard to find. From 1950 to 1974 the number of profit-sharing plans in the United States doubled every five years. The pace slackened a bit due to the uncertainties caused by ERISA legislation after 1974, but then picked up again, and there are now more than 360,000 companies in the United States with various kinds of profit-sharing plans in which more than 20 million employees participate. Profit-sharing plans are now in effect in about one of every four manufacturing companies, one of three retailing and wholesaling corporations, and about four of every ten banks.

Profit-sharing has a long history in the United States. The first plan was set up by Albert Gallatin at his glassworks in New Geneva, Pennsylvania, in the year 1797. Gallatin was secretary of the Treasury under President Thomas Jefferson, and a man of large vision. Through profit sharing he dreamed of a society which would extend the principles of democracy from the political field into the economic life of the newly founded American republic. If the number of profit-sharing plans keeps on growing—more than 20,000 new plans have been formed each year in recent years—Gallatin's dream may yet become a reality in the United States.

Some major American corporations have had profit-sharing plans for nearly a century. Colonel William C. Procter set up the Procter & Gamble plan in 1887. Eastman Kodak, Sears Roebuck, Harris Trust & Savings Bank, and Johnson Wax Co. all set up their plans between 1910 and 1920. Other big companies with profit-sharing plans include manufacturers such as Texas Instruments and Burlington Industries, retailers like Carter Hawley Hale, banks such as Manufacturers Hanover Corp. and First National Bank of Chicago, and mining concerns such as Mapco Inc.

The Profit Sharing Council of America (20 N. Wacker Drive, Chicago, IL 60606) has 1,300 member firms employing 1.75 million profit-sharing employees. The companies range from newly founded family enterprises to the world's largest retailers. The Council has been in business since 1947 researching the impact of profit-sharing on the American economy—employee motivation and productivity, job security, labor-management relations, capital accumulation, retirement income, and the quality of work life.

"It would be difficult," the Council says, "to overstate the impact of profit-sharing plans' investments on the financial vigor of the nation. The investment and reinvestment of some $175 billion of profit-sharing assets provide broad and sturdy support to financial markets."

A number of studies over the years have shown that companies with profit-sharing plans tend to outperform companies without such plans. One study, by Bion B. Howard of Northwestern University, examined the results of 202 companies in two periods, 1948–1966 and 1958–1977, and found that the profit sharers generally outperformed the others. Another study of profit sharing in thirty-eight large companies, by Bert L. Metzger, president of the Profit Sharing Research Foundation, found that in the 1973–1976 period, these thirty-eight companies—which included manufacturers, retailers and others—consistently outperformed comparable companies with no profit-sharing plans.

Metzger remarked that "it makes sense that employees will more likely strive for excellence if they have a direct stake in the results."

The question is, how much of a stake in the results? You are not going to be all that motivated if your company offers you and your fellow employees only a 1% share in profits. Different companies have different ways of figuring how much of their profits they are going to give their employees under the profit-sharing plan. Some companies have fixed formula plans in which they share a fixed percentage of profits, such as 25% of profits before taxes. These are likely to be the more reliable plans. Others have discretionary plans, in which the company directors decide each year what percentage of profits are to be shared with employees. This method is used particularly by small companies that have widely varying capital needs and widely fluctuating profits from one year to another. You would be wise not to count your chickens before they are hatched in budgeting your expenses if you are in this kind of plan.

Yet other plans are a combination of the previous two methods, in which the company agrees to share a stated percentage of profits, plus an extra discretionary amount to be determined by the directors if the company has a particularly good year.

Anyway the bottom line is: how much of a company's profits go into its profit-sharing plan? Hewitt Associates, an independent consulting firm, made a survey in 1985 of 529 companies with profit-sharing plans that were members of the Profit Sharing Council of America. It found that the average company contributed 24.1% of its net profits to the profit-sharing plan. This came to 8.8% of the covered payroll, so that the average employee was sharing in nearly one-quarter of his company's profits and thus getting an 8.8% bonus on top of his salary.

211

This is obviously a valuable benefit, but it does not benefit every employee equally. Most companies parcel out the funds in proportion to each employee's salary. A $40,000-a-year supervisor gets twice as much as a $20,000-a-year clerk, for example.

There are also different kinds of profit-sharing plans. The most common, about 80% of all plans, is the deferred plan, in which the benefits are not paid out immediately in cash but accumulated in a trust fund. Each employee piles up gradually increasing rights each year he works until he is fully vested, and he or his survivors collect whatever benefits he is entitled to when he leaves the company, is disabled, retires, or dies.

According to the Profit Sharing Council, company contributions to deferred profit-sharing plans average somewhere between 9% and 10% of payroll, but may range up to 15%. This tends to be the top because it is the legal limit of the company's tax deductibility under a deferred plan.

About 60% of these plans allow participants to make additional voluntary contributions to the profit-sharing plan, and a few even require such contributions.

In the cash plan, as opposed to the deferred plan, the company's contribution is paid out directly to employees at stated periods, usually annually. Two other types of plans are hybrids of the deferred and cash plans. In combination plans, part of the company's contribution is deferred and the rest is distributed immediately in cash. In combination option plans, you have some leeway as an employee in deciding yourself how much to take in cash and how much should go into the deferred plan for your retirement.

To old-timers who have seen the damage that inflation can do over the years, and to believers in the here and now who agree with Omar Khayyam's philosophical advice to "take the cash and let the credit go," the cash plan may seem the best bet. But the deferred plan is not only a nest egg for your retirement years. It can also give you a boost during your working years, particularly when you need money to buy a home or when you face a medical emergency or when you have to put a child through college. Many deferred plans allow you to make partial withdrawals during your working years, or to take a loan with your plan as collateral, in order to meet hardship situations. According to the Hewitt survey, about 80% of all deferred plans allow withdrawals for unanticipated financial hardships.

Usually you have to work at the company for a year before joining the profit-sharing plan, but some plans have no waiting period. Some stipulate a minimum age of twenty-one, but most have no age requirement. Your rights to benefits are either granted full and immediate vesting—which is obviously the best for you—or else build up gradually over the years until you are fully vested after working for the company for five, ten, or fifteen years.

Since there are more than 360,000 different company profit-sharing plans, most of our comments so far have been made in the most general terms. But one good example is worth a thousand generalities. So if you have been dozing off, here is a question to wake you up: would you rather retire from your company with $15,300 a year in company-provided benefits, or with nothing a year?

The question arises when we take the example of one outstanding profit-sharing plan, that of Signode Industries, a manufacturer of packaging products based in Glenview, Illinois. This example is historical, symbolic, and, like MCI's ESOP, it has a sting in the tail.

We are back in the 1970s. Signode's 4,000 employees are eligible to join the plan after six months on the job. The company contributes 30% of its profits, and employees can chip in another 10% of their earnings if they want to. Participants have 50% vesting immediately, and this rises to 100% after fifteen years, or whenever the employee dies, is disabled, or reaches the age of sixty. One hundred percent vesting means that none of the benefits will be forfeited for any reason. While he is working, an employee can withdraw part of his money to buy a house, reduce his mortgage, pay medical or educational expenses—but only twice during his career. The plan is of the deferred type, and its assets are invested in a mixture of common stocks, including Signode stock, and fixed-income securities. On retirement, an employee can take the money in a lump sum or in annual or monthly instalments.

"At Signode," says Bert Metzger in his 1978 study of profit sharing at thirty-eight large companies, "a participant with thirty-five years of profit-sharing participation who retired at a final pay of $14,466, received $127,752 in profit sharing—an annuity equivalent of $15,300 a year."

This is not only better than the nothing a year this employee would have received if there had been no profit-sharing plan at Signode. It is also better, according to Metzger's calculations, "than the $6,582 that he would have received from a standard pension plan." To be precise, 233% better than the average pension plan.

However, if you pick your employer properly, you don't even have to forgo the pension. The study by Hewitt Associates found that 28% of companies offering deferred profit-sharing plans also provided pension plans.

So add a $6,582 pension to a $15,300 annuity from a deferred profit-sharing plan and you get $21,882 a year. Add on to this the benefits due from Social Security. Add also whatever income the employee has been able to accumulate from his own private investments. And remember that all this is calculated from the income of a person who retired in 1978 at a final pay of $14,446 per year.

This person, supported by a profit-sharing plan and a pension plan, is much better off when he retires than he was when he was working.

To be prudent, fair, and even pessimistic, Metzger notes in his study that not all deferred profit-sharing

plans end up as well as Signode's did when he made his study. But he estimated that if a company consistently contributes 8% to 10% of employees' pay into a deferred profit-sharing plan, and if the investment return on this contribution over the years ranges from 6% to 10%, "participants should receive enough in profit-sharing income, complemented by Social Security, to adequately fund their retirement."

And now for the O. Henry short-story ending to this tale of Signode's profit-sharing plan. It is now 1987, Signode has been taken over by Illinois Tool Works, and all good things come to an end—even the company you work for, the things it believes in, and the benefits it offers. ITW does not believe in the profit-sharing concept, and the Signode profit-sharing plan was terminated December 31, 1986. The profit-sharing trust will distribute benefits as participants leave the company. But new employees are not covered. They are offered a pension plan instead.

Pension Plans: Old-Age Security at Up to 100% Off

Pension plans. A subject one tends to shrug off as remote, complicated, arcane, and inherently boring. A subject moreover that one can't really do much about.

And yet a noncontributory pension plan, where your employer pays everything and you contribute nothing could be the best investment you ever make. Its cost you is absolutely nothing, and it could be the foundation for a comfortable old age.

Your employer has no obligation to provide you with a pension plan, and many in fact do not. This is not factor that usually stands foremost in your mind when you are young and looking for a job, but it could be crucial to your later years, so keep it in mind in evaluating job offers, particularly as you grow older. And look in

215

the details. Some pension plans are a lot better than others.

Whether your employer's pension plan is a good deal for you depends basically on how much money the company puts in and how much you put in. If you contribute the bulk of the funds, you might be better off investing the money on your own. You would then have full control of your money and avoid the bureaucratic rules and restrictions on how the eventual benefits are to be paid out. If the company chips in with half the total contributions, you might figure that you are getting an investment at a 50% discount, and reckon that such a bargain outweighs the other disadvantages. And a noncontributory plan is of course all pure gravy for you.

This matter of a company pension is really crucial. Most Americans can expect a drastic decline in their income when they retire. If they have no savings or other sources of private income or family support, they can look forward to an old age of bare survival on Social Security payments. So a private company pension plan could be the most important investment of your lifetime, making the difference between retiring in poverty and retiring in reasonable comfort.

The fact is, however, that at present only about half the civilian work force is covered by private pension plans—about 51.5 million out of 99 million workers— and many of those who are covered may end up getting precious little out of their plans.

"Half of all those who are working for an employer that does have a pension plan are never going to be entitled to their benefits because they leave their jobs before they vest," said Senator John Heinz of Pennsylvania during the tax-reform-law hearings in August 1986.

One reason for this is the mobility of American society. Americans tend to job-hop more than any other people in the world, and this does them no good at all when they have to stay with one company for at least several years in order to qualify for benefits under its

pension plan (to be fully vested, in the jargon of the specialists).

About 42% of American workers are in jobs that can be expected to last up to five years, and another 15% are in jobs that will last five to ten years. So altogether, about 57% of all workers are in jobs that will last ten years or less. Since most pension plans in recent years required a minimum of ten years before pension benefits were vested (nonforfeitable by early departure) this meant that well over half of all American workers have been in jobs that would not lead to a pension even if they contributed to one.

Fortunately, the tax reform law of 1986 promised major improvements to America's prospective pensioners. Under the new law, the minimum period you must stick with one company to be fully vested in its pension plan is reduced to only five years.

This reduces the percentage of workers who are left without pension rights, but not by much. The number left out is still more than 40%. And in any case the new law is not going to benefit job-hoppers to any great extent because the size of the pension benefits usually depends on the length of service and the salary level of the last few years in an employee's career. Most of the 1986 law's changes, moreover, were not intended to go into effect until December 31, 1988, to allow companies time to adjust.

Nevertheless, in the long run the 1986 tax reform law promises some major improvements for America's future pensioners. According to the American Association of Retired Persons, the changes mean that 68% of Americans will be covered by private pension plans between the years 2011 and 2020, instead of 59%, and their pensions will be 22% higher than they would otherwise have been.

Americans miss out on private pension plan benefits for other reasons than job-hopping. One reason is the way their company plan is structured. Some plans, for

217

instance, are "integrated" with Social Security. This means that some or all of the Social Security retirement benefits are deducted from the company's pension plan benefits. This is probably the worst kind of pension plan, and in the economic environment of the 1970s and early 1980s it probably qualified as "cruel and unusual punishment." It is particularly cruel when inflation runs riot, because Social Security benefits are indexed to keep pace with inflation whereas practically all private pension plans are not. The result of this is that when the Promises Shpromises Corporation says it will pay you a pension of $800 a month thirty years from now, and in the meanwhile inflation has pushed your Social Security retirement benefits up to $1,000 a month, the Promises Shpromises Corporation is not going to pay you any pension at all.

This is another area where the 1986 tax reform law improved the situation somewhat. It prevents an employer from reducing your retirement benefits by more than 50% when taking Social Security benefits into account. Nevertheless, it does not solve the problem completely. So when evaluating job offers, give preference to the company pension plan that stands on its own, without regard to Social Security or any other outside benefits. And if you are offered a private company pension plan indexed to inflation—we haven't come across any, but there may be some springing up out there—give it preference over any other plan.

Inflation inflicts such a disastrous injustice on people with fixed incomes, particularly old people who are no longer able to fend for themselves, that the indexing of private pension plans to inflation may well be the next major reform in this area. In the meanwhile, as long as they are not so indexed, the importance you attach to your company's plan should increase as you grow older—on a scale from 0 to 100, shall we say from 10 at age twenty-five to 100 at age sixty. If you still have forty years of work ahead of you, the chances are that what you pay into the pension plan yourself, or what the company pays in for you, in the early years of your career is not going to be worth much or count for much in the final evaluation of your pension rights. When you are sixty, the input of the last few years will count for a lot, and the bogey of inflation will by then have only five or ten years to nibble away at your pension rights instead of forty years.

One crucial point that you may tend to overlook is that your private company pension does not cover your family; it covers you. The law considers your pension to be yours alone, not the joint property of your spouse. So if you should die, your widow or widower will not automatically collect your pension benefits. Most plans allow you to handle this problem in advance, however. After a certain age you can stipulate that your surviving spouse is to receive your benefits, which are usually paid at a reduced rate. This is an option you will have to face anyway if you reach retirement age alive. How much of a pension is your spouse going to receive if you should be the first to die after retiring?

If you do not want to leave your spouse without any pension at all, as presumably you do not, you can stipulate that your pension payments continue for both your lifetimes. This will be at a reduced rate, of course, the amount of the reduction depending on the age of the spouse—the younger the spouse the bigger the reduction. Most plans give you several different ways of doing this, such as 50% or 75% or 100% of the joint benefits to the surviving spouse.

If you are over fifty, the age bracket in which many plans allow you to assign benefits to your spouse, you should ask yourself: if I drop dead of a heart attack this very minute, what kind of a pension will my spouse receive? If you don't know the answer, make an appointment with your company's pension plan administrator tomorrow morning and do whatever has to be done.

One major flaw in all pension plans is a problem

common to all collective investments designed to cover hundreds or even thousands of employees. The plans are necessarily rough-hewn, not precisely cut to cover the peculiar circumstances of each individual participant. What is the surviving-spouse benefit in the case of a man who was married to one woman for ten years, to a second woman for three years, and to a third for twenty? And will he be allowed to channel the benefits to wife number two, as he wishes to do, in view of the fact that she is disabled by a stroke?

The biggest potential flaw of all in a company pension plan, of course, is the possibility that the company may go bankrupt. What happens to its pension plan then? Up to 1974 it was just too bad for you if your company went belly-up and couldn't continue paying the benefits. In that year, however, the government set up the Pension Benefit Guaranty Corporation, which now protects participants in private pension plans in the same way the Federal Deposit Insurance Corporation protects bank depositors if their bank goes under. Nevertheless, be aware that the PBGC does not cover all pension plans. Those paid for by union dues are excluded, for example. So check the booklet describing your plan. Whether it is government-insured or not could be vitally important to you later on if your company gets into difficulties.

The PBGC currently protects the retirement incomes of more than 38 million participants in about 112,000 private pension plans. The Corporation is now responsible for paying guaranteed pension benefits earned by more than 177,000 participants in about 1,200 terminated plans. The premium for this insurance is paid by the pension plan administrators and is currently $8.50 per participating employee per year.

If you have any doubts about your plan's insured status, the address to contact is the Coverage and Inquiries Branch, Insurance Operations Department, Pension Benefit Guaranty Corporation, 2020 K Street, N.W., Washington, DC 20006-1806.

220

All the problems with private pension plans we have described above led to a fundamental reform law in 1974, which among other things gave birth to the PBGC. Formally known as the Employment Retirement Security Act (ERISA), it was nicknamed by some unhappy employers who objected to all the extra paper work, Every Ridiculous Idea Since Adam.

ERISA spells out your rights if you are covered by a pension plan. You should be given a booklet explaining the plan's provisions in plain English, not gobbledygook. You should be told how much of a pension you will get and at what age. These plans are known as defined benefit plans, which means they are obliged to state precisely how much the benefits will be, and then pay those benefits, neither more nor less. You are entitled to ask how your pension plan contributions are being invested, which should be detailed in the plan's annual report. If you think the money is being invested in risky ventures or mishandled (there have been some nasty examples of this, particularly in big union-run pension plans), complain to the U.S. Department of Labor, Office of Communications and Public Services, Pension, Welfare and Benefit Programs, 200 Constitution Avenue, N.W., Room S4522, Washington, DC 20216.

If you think you have been unfairly denied a pension, or fired, or discriminated against so that the plan won't have to pay you a pension, you can sue in state or federal court. One organization that can offer help in such cases is the National Senior Citizens Law Center, 1200 Fifteenth Street, N.W., Washington, DC 20005. Another is the Pension Rights Center, 1346 Connecticut Avenue, N.W., Washington, DC 20036.

With the pension law reforms of recent years and the PBGC's insurance coverage you now have a better chance than ever before of actually getting a decent pension from your company's plan. But when you do retire you are still dogged by the same old bogey of inflation. The pension of $10,000 a year that seemed adequate in

1987 when added to Social Security benefits and other personal income may well be reduced to a pittance by 1997 by the constant erosion of inflation.

As long as your pension is not adjusted to inflation—and the best that some companies do is offer some voluntary increases now and again—your only real protection is to continue working as long as you can.

Employee Savings Plans And the Full Works

There are companies that offer not merely one of the employee benefit plans outlined in this chapter, but a full panoply of them.

Here is perhaps the prime example of what it can mean to work for a company that enables you to turn your job into a lifetime investment. International Business Machines is not only the world's biggest computer company, and probably America's most successful corporation, it is also a standout in its concern for its employees, which might well be a major reason for its success.

"IBM's retirement plan, like its benefits program," says the company, "has long been one of the best in industry. IBM's leadership in this area is a matter of considerable company pride. It provides a good, solid foundation income, a base for retirement."

The company pays the entire cost of the pension benefits. This is not all, however. IBM provides other plans for its employees to expand savings and accumulate capital.

One is the IBM Tax Deferred Savings Plan, through which an employee can invest up to 8% of his or her annual compensation in five different investment vehicles: a money market fund, an index fund, a guaranteed income fund, or two equity funds. IBM contributes 30 cents for each dollar of the first 5% put into this plan.

222

All this money is excluded from the employee's annual taxable income and will not be taxed until withdrawal at or after retirement.

Then there is the IBM Employees Stock Purchase Plan, in which IBM people can buy IBM stock at a 15% discount. They may put as much as 10% of their eligible compensation into IBM stock in this way.

Set out as above in general terms, it all sounds very dry and abstruse. It comes more vividly to life when you take the case of Jonathan Livingston (who is based on a real, live, middle-level IBM employee, although his name and some other details have been changed here to maintain his privacy). Livingston, a widower, retired at age sixty-five in 1986 at a final salary of $40,000 after thirty years with IBM. Throughout his career he participated to the fullest extent possible in all the IBM plans offered. In his final years with the company this absorbed more than 20% of his income.

But this is what it all came to: a pension of $14,000 a year; $11,600 in his deferred savings plan (not bad for a plan that was first offered in 1983); and the crowning glory, 1,716 shares of IBM from his Employees Stock Purchase Plan. At the current price of $120 each, these shares were worth $205,920.

After his retirement party there was one last parting gift. Livingston planned to study Elizabethan drama at a nearby college, and IBM reimbursed him $2,500 toward the cost of his studies under its Retirement Education Assistance Plan.

Livingston had two further IBM benefits that younger employees will not enjoy, thanks to our legislators in Washington. IBM started an Employees Voluntary Retirement Savings Plan in 1982 under which he could make voluntary contributions of up to $2,000 a year and invest the money in a selection of five different investment funds. In four years he piled up $12,210 in this plan. The other was an IBM Employees Stock Ownership Plan (ESOP), started in 1981, in which the company offered IBM stock without cost. The number of shares each employee received depended on his or her salary, commissions, and cash awards earned during each year.

Both the Voluntary Retirement Savings Plan and the ESOP were terminated at the end of 1986 due to the tax reform law of that year. So Livingston got only $900 out of his ESOP before it succumbed to the zeal of lawmakers who set out to simplify the tax system, plug tax loopholes for the rich, and benefit the American working class. They somehow ended up complicating such simple matters as an employee's W-4 standard deductions form, penalizing hardworking middle-class Americans, and snuffing out benefit programs of generous employers like IBM.

Nevertheless, with an array of benefits such as those provided by top-notch American companies you might indeed consider yourself a full-time investor, on the job as well as in whatever dabbling you do on your own time.

IRA Gone? Here's the 401(k) Solution

And while we are on the subject of your own personal investments, perhaps you too were one of the victims of the tax reform law of 1986, which dealt a nasty blow to many employed people by abolishing the major advantage of their Individual Retirement Account (IRA) if they work for a company that provides a pension plan. The reform meant that employees covered by a company pension plan making more than $25,000 a year ($40,000 if married) could no longer take the $2,000 IRA investment off their taxable income.

But there is still an alternative, and it is even better than the lost IRA. The key is whether your company has a 401(k) plan. If it does not, pressure your management to introduce one. The 401(k) works somewhat like an

IRA, and it allows you to stash away as much as $7,000 a year instead of the IRA's measly $2,000. And in many cases there is an even better feature: the employer chips in with part of that $7,000.

The 401(k) plans were first allowed in 1978, and they are now the fastest-growing employee benefit in American history. As many as 19 million Americans are eligible for them. In most 401(k) plans the employer matches part or even all of employee savings.

The 401(k) plans did not escape the ravages of the 1986 tax reform entirely, but their previous limit—you could knock off as much as $30,000 a year off your income with a 401(k)—was so incredibly generous that its reduction to $7,000 still leaves a benefit so liberal that most people don't even make enough money to take full advantage of it.

The way it works is that your employer withholds as much as $7,000 from your yearly pay and contributes whatever it is going to chip in, and this is invested in your 401(k) plan. If you are making $40,000 a year, your taxable income is thus reduced to $33,000, and the remaining $7,000, plus the income it earns, sits there untaxed until you retire. The 401(k) stands for Section 401(k) of the Internal Revenue Code, which considers your contribution a pretax reduction in salary.

Your 401(k) may be invested in thrift plans, profit-sharing plans, and various other options such as life and health insurance and other benefits.

Any employer which does not offer you a 401(k) plan is not doing its best for you in keeping Uncle Sam off your back.

The Last Resort—Uncle Sam

If you are already in your fifties and you have never given much thought to your retirement plans, you may have concluded by now that this whole chapter comes much too late for you—you should have been thinking about your retirement years in your twenties like the industrious ant instead of fiddling the years away like the feckless grasshopper. Fear not, however. As the poet said, "Grow old with me; the best is yet to come." The best in this case being good old Uncle Sam.

To come down from ESOPs to prosaic facts, you should think about getting a job with the federal government. Too old for that at fifty-five? Not necessarily so. We know people who got federal jobs at age fifty-nine. The U.S. government has laws against age discrimination for job-seekers, it enforces them against private employers, and it can scarcely avoid honoring its own rules in the job market. Besides, the government bureaucrat who hires you is likely to be somewhat less concerned about the financial consequences of his hiring decisions than a private employer would.

Now, once you have got this fellow to give you a job, this is your situation, according to the Employee Benefit Research Institute, a Washington-based organization that looks into these matters:

Federal Pension: civil service employees are covered by their own retirement income program. Full civil service pension benefits are generally provided to retirees who satisfy one of several possible criteria: (1) age fifty-five with thirty years of service, (2) age sixty with twenty years of service, or (3) age sixty-two with five years of service.

In other words, the older you are when you join the government work force the less time you have to work to qualify for a pension. If you get a government job at fifty-seven, five years will do.

This is not all, though. Your civil service pension is supposed to be funded out of a 7% deduction from your paycheck plus another 7% contribution from Uncle Sam. The pension benefits became so generous over the years, however, that this was not enough to pay the bill. The government then did what it usually does—it hit the U.S.

226

taxpayer for the difference. The Employee Benefit Research Institute estimates that in 1986 "general revenue financing" for the civil service retirement system exceeded $20 billion.

What this statement means in fact is that John Q. Taxpayer is chipping in $20 billion a year to round out your federal pension benefits and those of 2.7 million other participants in the civil service pension plan.

This involuntary contribution of your fellow citizens—which incidentally mushroomed twentyfold from only $1 billion in 1970—is likely to grow even further in the years to come. The reason is that federal pensions are fully indexed to cost-of living increases twice a year. For a time, due to a quirk in the calculation process, federal retirees' pensions were being cranked up at an even higher rate than the consumer price index they were based on.

There is not in all probability a private pension plan in the country that can match any of this. The snag, of course, is that you first have to get yourself a job with the federal government. But this may not be such a big snag as it appears at first. The Federal Jobs Digest (P.O. Box 594, Millwood, NY 10456), a biweekly, privately owned publication, is one of several periodicals that list thousands of federal government job offerings. A three-month subscription costs $39.

In late 1986 the departments of state, defense, justice, and many other federal agencies were hiring 20,000 people a month nationwide. The job openings were in every occupation and salary range. They included such out-of-the-ordinary specialties as autopsy assistant, cemetery caretaker, and psychology technician, as well as store manager and other prosaic occupations. All this, be it noted, was at a time when President Reagan was trying to cut back on a "bloated federal bureaucracy."

There is one last point. If you should get a civil service job, you may not want to retire at sixty-two. Most civilian employees of the federal government have been exempt from forced retirement at any age since 1978. As long as you can still do your job and want to do it, Uncle Sam may be stuck with you for as long as you both shall live.

The rest of us who do not work for the government had to wait until 1986 for a law against mandatory retirement that gives us the right to continue working until we drop dead of old age. At which point, of course, most of the job-related investment discussed in this chapter becomes redundant.

Footnote: For further information on pensions, Social Security, 401(k) plans, and retirement planning in general, the Employee Benefit Research Institute (2121 K Street, N.W., Washington, DC 20037-2121) has available some excellent books and other literature.

CONCLUSION

NO-COST/ LOW-COST INVESTORS— SKEPTICS YES, CYNICS NO

Well, that just about concludes our tour of the financial-services jungle. Saw some frightening creatures, didn't we? There was the investment broker who wants to be a "partner" in our stock market ventures while we take all the risk. Who can forget the mutual funds that want to hit us for sales charges, redemption charges, management fees, expense fees, even the cost of selling fund shares to other people we have never met? And those bankers who offer to borrow our money at a low interest rate, lend it back at a high interest rate, and charge us a long list of fees for the privilege?

It's enough to make one cynical, maybe even paranoid. But that hasn't been our intention. We believe a no-cost/low-cost investor can and should be *skeptical* without being cynical, *suspicious* but not paranoid. When we subject today's financial services industry to a close inspection, we find nothing that's really very surprising. In the main, it is made up simply of people acting, like the rest of us, in their own interest. Anywhere there is a lot of money to be made, we are bound to find some low-life types, scoundrels, frauds, and thieves. That's one of many reasons why the game of investing and managing money favors the careful and the well informed.

But if we encountered any big surprise along the way, we think it was this: there are, in fact, many ways to put our money to work productively these days that won't divert a lot of that money into somebody else's pocket. Maybe those strategies don't get much publicity or advertising, but that's only natural. What bank or broker or fund manager is going to spend money promoting something that won't bring in any revenue?

In the course of this book, we have seen perfectly practical ways to invest in the stock market at little or no commission cost, or even at a discount from the going market price. We have seen that there are mutual funds—even if they represent only a small percentage of the overall fund population—that put almost all our money to work for us rather than their managers. In the obscure little world of closed-end funds, we've discovered a way to buy into a portfolio of securities at well below their going market price, if our timing is right. Our doting Uncle in Washington makes it possible for us to invest for safety and income without paying a nickel in commissions or fees. It may be a little tougher in banking, but there too we can avoid a lot of unnecessary expenses by asking the right questions and adopting some well-informed strategies. Lastly, we have seen that financial fringe benefits offered by many employers can help us significantly in our efforts to provide ourselves with financial security in our later years.

What's especially remarkable to us is that many no-cost/low-cost investment opportunities seem to offer the hope of generous rewards without exposure to any particular out-of-the-ordinary risks. As we said several times in the preceding pages of this book, we have no answers to the riddle of the future in the world economy or the

231

financial markets. If there is a bear market in stocks or bonds next week, next year, next decade, any investor—no-cost/low-cost or not—is likely to lose money. Win or lose, however, we hope we have helped you to play the game at the lowest possible price of admission.

I N D E X

238